NORTH WRITERS II

NORTH WRITERS II

OUR PLACE
IN THE WOODS

John Henricksson, editor

Foreword by Paul Gruchow

University of Minnesota Press
Minneapolis
London

Published by the University of Minnesota Press
111 Third Avenue South, Suite 290
Minneapolis, MN 55401-2520

Printed in the United States of America on acid-free paper

Library of Congress Cataloging-in-Publication Data

North writers II : our place in the woods / John Henricksson, editor ;
   Foreword by Paul Gruchow.
      p.   cm.
   ISBN 0-8166-2903-X (pb : alk. paper)
      1. Natural history—Authorship.   2. Natural history literature.
   I. Henricksson, John.
   QH14.N68   1997
   508—dc21   96-51647

The University of Minnesota is an equal-opportunity educator and employer.

For three blessings—Lisa, Marnie, and Ann

Contents

NORTH COUNTRY LIVING

THE LIVES AROUND US

IN THE ELEMENTS

Foreword

Paul Gruchow

It is easy to trivialize the idea of place. You need simply point out that every creature, animal or vegetable, occupies a place and is attached to it either literally, as in the case of a tree or a barnacle, or has some instinct to defend it, as in the case of a rat or a human; and to add that no known virtue derives from place, despite the odd twentieth-century-American presumption that people who hail from populous or famous places are likely to be smarter, prettier, and more sophisticated than people with obscure addresses. Hence, one might be tempted to conclude, place is a petty matter. But this is like saying that oxygen is a substance of no account because even worms depend upon it, or that sex is of no human significance because even thistles engage in it.

When place is discounted as an idea, the mistake lies in presuming that it is a mere thing, identifiable by a set of geographical coordinates, or that attachment to a place consists of some kind of perverse love affair with the stones in the driveway, the shingles on the shanty roof, and the pigweeds in the yard. In fact, location is the least important quality of a place. A place exists as much in time as in space and so has both a history and a future. Like the universe itself, a place is at least four-dimensional; any place is both central and infinite. A place, that is, is not only a pair of geographical coordinates or a collection of particular objects situated within them, the love of which would be quite absurd, but a set of relationships that locate the self in the world and affirm the connections between that self and the rest of creation, inanimate as well as animate, and not only to the presently living but also to everything that has lived or is yet to be born. A person without a sense of place is literally lost, not only in space but also in time.

I do not mean to discount the power of landscape in itself to inform our lives. One morning recently, on a walk along the Idaho-Montana border, I encountered two teenagers. They were in high sagebrush desert, open country extending to the horizons in every direction, uninterrupted by so much as a single tree. The few roads in that country were faint jeep tracks. I had tried to follow one of them, significant enough to be marked on a topographic map, and it had vanished after a couple of miles into the sparse cover of sagebrush, rabbitbrush, and needle grass, and so it was that, wandering cross-country, I came into the company of the young cowboys.

The road, for all I could tell, emerged from nowhere and led nowhere. I had last seen a house three days earlier; it had been abandoned and was falling in upon itself. The landscape I was walking is part of that vast central region of the United States where the human population averages fewer than two persons per square mile. Into this austere place, from over a rocky hilltop, suddenly appeared the two boys on horseback, dressed in cowboy boots, denim jeans, western shirts, and leather chaps. I watched them enter a draw, expertly round up fifty cattle, and drive the herd through a pair of gates into new pasture. Then the boys turned without a gesture of acknowledgment, galloped up the hillside, and disappeared over the horizon as quickly as they came. I climbed the hill myself, for I was going in their direction. When I came to the top of it, I could see no sign of them, nor any clue suggesting where they might have headed. It was as if they had melted into the earth or ascended to heaven.

How, I wondered, did those boys see the world? I could not imagine myself living in such starkness and isolation, encountering the world day in and day out at the pace of a horse, existing so close to the overweening sky and its raging moods as to have something of a bird's relationship to the solid earth, accustomed to a society with many more cattle than people, awakening in the night not to the sounds of sirens or laughter in the streets or honking horns but to the yipping of coyotes. What would you make, if you grew up in such country, of the common assertion that nature is but a trivial distraction from the weighty affairs of humanity?

The Minnesota northland of this book imposes its own demands upon the human imagination. It is in its way as closed as the desert country of the high plains is open—a landscape of bedrock ridges and swampy or boggy swales, of streams tumbling through deep ravines and lakes hiding in dense forests. The north country embraces Minnesota's highest point, an old mountain, from which there is no view. It is a land of elemental forces, of water and rock, of ice and fire, a youthful landscape in which the scour marks of the glaciers still show. Its long winters are secluding, its brief summers invaded by the hordes of tourists who swoop in with the mosquitoes and the black flies. Most of the ways of making a living in the north country—mining, logging, fishing, tourism—are extractive, exhausting people as much as natural wealth.

As if by way of compensation for the hardships it imposes, the north country is also ravishingly beautiful and, in its rawness, exciting. This would seem to be a rule of nature: the more alluring a landscape is, the harder it is to survive there.

"The old-timers," Sheila Packa writes, "talk about winters they've known, storms and shipwrecks, the bridges washing out, and thick fogs. Never love."

"Death was a way of life here, from gunshot, from freezing, from wandering off in the middle of the winter, from despair," says Kent Nerburn. "People killed to live, and they lived to kill."

"I'm looking at this still vaguely Cretaceous landscape," Steven R. Downing says of the mine dumps along the Iron Range, "at what grows on the dumps now: birch and aspen mainly. Spindly aspen, growing up either in dense impenetrable thickets or one cartoony tree every thousand feet, up from roots like steel wire. Spindly birch, seemingly without the energy to make branches and leaves. The impression is of bones, shinbones and thighbones especially, stuck on end into the purple-orange hills."

"Some poet, a long time ago, said, 'If winter comes, can spring be far behind?' You bet it can, and especially this year," Elnora Bixby writes.

What doesn't kill you will make you stronger, the old saying goes. Believing that is a point of pride in these essays. Let others live on the abundant and tedious plains or coddled in a luxury of humanity in the metropolises of the coasts. We north country people have chosen a harder, lonelier way and have not only survived but learned to love the challenge.

There is truth in this sentiment. Learning, like heat, requires resistance. Our deepest convictions arise in response not to what we know but to what we oppose and try to find reasons for opposing. Love and hatred are not opposites but sides of the same coin; both stand in opposition to indifference. Persist in a landscape that habitually conspires to kill you, as the north country does, and you cannot be indifferent to it; you will come eventually either to love or to hate it.

Thus Carol Bly's trenchant argument: real love of a place manifests itself not in moony sentiments about laughing loons or moody fogs wafting up from morning lakes but in righteous anger against the forces that would destroy such places and in the savvy engagement of their enemies. The look of love is steel-eyed, not teary. It finds beauty in what no one else has noticed, as the poet Tom Hennen reminds us:

> It's easy to love a deer
> But try to pick out insects and scrawny trees
> to care about.
> Love the puddle of lukewarm water
> From last week's rain.
> Leave the mountains alone for now.
> Also the clear lakes surrounded by pines.
> People are already lined up to admire them.
> Get close to the things that slide away in the dark.
> Think of the frost
> That will crack our bones eventually.
> Be grateful even for the boredom
> That sometimes seems to involve the whole world,
> Sometimes just the grass.

There are not, in fact, many loons or Bambis in this volume, a testament to its authenticity, since it certifies the kind of love that is hard-won, anchored in the roots rather than in the showy bangles of the landscape. Anyway, loons, like tourists, are fair-weather residents.

My own love is for the small farming communities of the prairies, places brimming with ugliness and not at all easy to admire, much less to love. When I drive through the rural Midwest, I am often revulsed by what I encounter—the stench of animal factories, of canneries and packing plants, the banality of the buildings, the decay of abandoned farmhouses and empty storefronts, the bathos of fiberglass cows and deer ornamenting sterile lawns, the weeds growing in sidewalk cracks. Then I come to a town where I know someone or where I once made a speech or visited a school or paused in a park, and that place, so like all the others, looks somehow different to me, lovelier, less fatally blemished, more welcoming. Even the slightest connection with a place alters it for the better, as the face a friend perceives is more beautiful than the one visible to a stranger, and at the same time admits a frankness that acknowledges its evils and shortcomings without excuse but not without forgiveness.

"I view it," says Captain Littlepage in Sarah Orne Jewett's *The Country of the Pointed Firs,*

> that a community narrows down and grows dreadful ignorant when it is shut up to its own affairs, and gets no knowledge of the outside world except from a cheap, unprincipled newspaper. In the old days, a good part o' the best men here knew a hundred ports and something of the way folks lived in them. They may not have had the best knowledge to carry with 'em sight-seein', but they were some acquainted with foreign lands and their laws, an' could see outside the battle for town clerk here in Dunnet; they got some sense o' proportion. Yes, they lived more dignified, and their houses were better within an' without.

This observation bears moral authority precisely because the author herself spent her life in a New England town quite like Dunnet and was devoted to it. Carol Bly and Barton Sutter both rightly assert that no virtue emanates from love of a particular place, but there is a virtue in writing about the place into which one has been assimilated, as the authors of this volume all do: by the license of membership in a community one has earned the right to reveal it, however affectionately, without a sugar coating.

The connections that these authors find to the north country are of three kinds: to the land itself, to those antecedents whose lives cannot be separated from the land, and to the nonhuman lives that share citizenship in it. These connections are distinct but indivisible, like the proverbial legs of a stool: without any one of them the stool will not stand.

The connection to the land largely consists in having come to terms with it, in accepting the inevitability and justness of its demands. We don't love places because they're readily lovable.

"For years my relationship with Koochiching was one of resignation," Bobbie Greiner writes. "I lived here, but I didn't always like it. . . . It is land that defies my patience with the shovel and rake. Cheap, $100-an-acre land that no one else wanted, land I've learned to love in spite of its stubbornness, in spite of myself."

Sharon Miltich: "The young cameraman . . . says he's working on a documentation project for the University of Minnesota, filming the decline of the Range. Unemployment, poverty, perseverance. A poet is heading up the project, he says. He is here to tell my story, a story that deserves to be told. 'What keeps you here?' he asks, all sad-eyed sincerity. 'I really want to know.' I shrug and tell him nothing."

"In winter," says Jana Studelska, "I examine my most humiliating traits. I grow tired of my bad habits, bored with my own excuses. I quit television, I lose weight, I vacuum walls, I start writing novels and stitching hopelessly intricate needlepoint patterns. The strength of my resolution is second only to weariness of my own bad company. I am always a better person after winter, because I know what makes me ugly, and I have faced it."

Often a bond with the land is forged through some kind of labor. Work, especially physical work, is the twentieth century's most underrated blessing. In being hoodwinked into believing that labor efficiency is the highest public good, we have not only let ourselves in for a great deal of tedious extra work, but we have deprived ourselves of the great consolations of labor, such as pleasure in sweating, the marvelous taste of cold water, joy in rest, and pride in having accomplished something tangible.

These consolations are learned very early. Sheila Packa remembers a young cousin who loved his saw so much that he slept with it in his crib; Anne M. Dunn remembers watching as a young girl for the box elders to begin to weep in the springtime, signaling the start of the sugar bush season; and Jeanne Grauman remembers going to the woods to cut a Christmas tree armed with a meat saw, in case she should meet a wolf along the way.

There is not much talk here, by light of the setting sun in the solitude of a wilderness lake, about discovering one's inner child, but there is a lot about gardening and cooking, making maple syrup, carpentry and mining, building stone walls: another sign of authenticity. We do not come to know landscapes passively. All scenery is unmemorable except as it is experienced through the hands and feet in labor.

Thus the classic vacation photograph: not the Grand Canyon but Aunt Emma and Uncle Bert standing in front of a sign that says "Grand Canyon." The photograph acknowledges the fact that, years later, Aunt Emma and Uncle Bert will not remember the Grand Canyon itself but only the experience of having gone there. One of the radical disjunctions of modern life is that most of us live in one place and work in another. The old connections between place and self, mediated by labor—connections still alive for the writers in this volume—are steadily being severed. In a sense, therefore, this is a volume of historical anthropology.

One day I came through the park near our house on my way home from work and found my eight-year-old daughter sitting on a tree stump weeping bitterly. I ran to her, trying to imagine what calamity had bestruck her. I held her in my arms for several minutes. She was too disconsolate to speak. Finally, between her sobs, she was able to tell me what had happened. City workers had come while she was at school and cut down the willow tree on whose stump she was sitting. It had been, indeed, quite a magnificent old tree, as furrowed and wizened as the face of an ancient woman. I did not know so until then, but it was my daughter's favorite tree, into whose broad limbs she had repaired when she was sad or lonely or in a dreamy mood. Losing it so suddenly and unexpectedly was as cruel to her as losing any person in her life.

Places matter not in grand and abstract ways, not as idealized landscapes, but in such particulars as we have come to know intimately, as my daughter had come to know that willow tree. We don't love prairies or mountains or the sea, but the prairie as it has often appeared from the vantage point of a particular erratic boulder, or the sea as seen from a particular point on a particular bay on certain moonlit nights, or one mountain as it has appeared to us from a certain deck on many cool mornings. Our attachment is not to places as points in space but to the accumulations of experience that we associate with them. Love of a place is the sum of a relationship. You love a place as you love yourself or another person. There is nothing sentimental or nostalgic about it except insofar as the love persists as a figment of the imagination beyond the termination of the relationship.

Barton Sutter has his Tischer Creek. He goes to it, he writes, "to wash away my worries, to rid myself of all my best ideas and fill up instead on images—dew in the grass, a bug on the water, sunshine on red rock—things that will sustain me when I go back to the world of cinder block and fluorescent lights where most of us work these days. Stuck with high-tech ugliness, I listen for the shush and whisper of a stream called Tischer Creek."

Marlon Davidson has his hill. "Even so minor an elevation of land as my hill," he writes of it, "seems to draw me there when I feel a need for quietness and reflection. The distances are soothing to my vision and I realize how I need to see a horizon, like a string long and straight, uncluttering my mind."

And Bobbie Greiner has a place in the woods where a white pine has been toppled by the wind, its upturned roots making a lacy fan. One of the branches of the old pine continues to live and by now has become a tree in its own right. "That tree is special to me," she says, "because it matters not how far its seed traveled before it took root. Nor does it matter where it came from, whether its parent stood one foot away, or miles. The important thing is that it did not perish when the wind storm blew it over—and that it found the one spot on earth in which to anchor itself. Like the pine, I am sustained by this place in northern Minnesota. . . . The circuitous route by which I arrived here is irrelevant. What matters is that I was fated to belong here."

One school of landscape photography ruthlessly eliminates from the frame any trace of human presence. The pictures that result are often ravishingly beautiful, as they could hardly help but be given that their subject is nature, but to my eye they are also sterile and distancing. There seems to me more disdain than love in them, just as it is ultimately demeaning to put a person on a pedestal. When you hate yourself, it is as difficult to love some part of nature as it is to love another human.

And, in any case, one of the great blessings of being bound to a place is that it links you to all that has gone before in that place, and especially to every human in its lineage. I have written elsewhere that home lies at the crossroads between history and heaven; there, the past and the future converge in the present. It is exhilarating and legitimating to be part of something so grandly continuous.

Matthew Miltich's cousin Ivo, who still lives in the village in Croatia where Miltich's grandmother was born, says something very beautiful about building stone walls that might stand as parable for the process by which a human connection with the land is also built. "You don't go out and build a wall," he says. "When you walk along the road, you pick up a stone. You put the stone in the wall. In this way, after five hundred years you have a wall."

Neither do you build a connection with the land by intention alone. You settle in a place and others join you; by and by you will have made a community, and if this community endures from one generation into the next, and the next, in five hundred years, maybe, the place and its people will have been conjoined. We European descendants occupying the North American landscape are still too new here to have built an indelible connection with the land. We still think of ourselves as imposters, as indeed in some ways we are; perhaps this is why we are prone to the destructive belief that our very presence defiles the land, that the only pure land is virgin land. One way to fight against this impulse is to savor the memories, as the authors of this volume do, of fathers and mothers, aunts and uncles, grandmothers and grandfathers whose spirits live in the places to which we are attached.

Peter Leschak's chickadee named Bob, John Henricksson's owls, Jane Whitledge's geese, Jim Brandenburg's wolves and ravens are also part of the great continuity of the north country; we share in such lives by virtue of our membership in the community of a place.

Brandenburg describes the complex relationship between ravens and wolves. "The wolf has been our companion," he writes. "And as a vital part of a fully functioning ecosystem, the wolf can serve as teacher, reminding us that two species sharing similar ecological niches might also share similar fates. If, one day, the wolf no longer finds the world a fit place in which to live, we may face a similar and inescapable destiny."

This idea has already become so familiar to most of us as to seem a bit trite, but its rediscovery is probably the most revolutionary and far-reaching intellectual development of the late twentieth century, as shattering of old complacencies as the news, once upon a time, that the universe does not revolve around the earth, or the ninteenth-century revelation that the work of natural creation on earth is ongoing and we humans are not necessarily its culmination.

Another of the seminal ideas of our century is Aldo Leopold's provocative suggestion that our moral development is as yet unfinished. In ecological terms, he argued, an ethic is a freedom we voluntarily relinquish in the interests of our long-term survival; the next stage in our moral development will be to understand that we have ethical obligations to the land and its creatures as much as to each other, obligations that limit our freedom to do whatever we will with land and wildlife so that we might secure the prospects of our own species.

We will need, of course, if we are to achieve this advanced stage of moral development, a new language—one that moves beyond the humanities' disinterestedness in mere nature and the clinical detachment of the sciences, one that admits of a passionate regard for land—and we will need, therefore, a new standard of literacy. In the future, a person who is ignorant of the expectations of the land will be as handicapped in society as one who cannot do sums or read and write.

This anthology moves toward a literacy of northern Minnesota. That is, ultimately, its great and good contribution.

Acknowledgments

Editing an anthology of contemporary regional nonfiction is an adventure in listening to the many voices of a living landscape. It is the land that defines and begets these voices. They are not always the loudest or most lyrical, but they are the truest, the heart voices.

In this collection there are professional writers with established reputations, "kitchen table" writers who feel strongly the need to write, hobby writers, retirees with a wish to reminisce, creative writing teachers, environmental activists and students who write with great feeling and promise. It is a complex harmony. The landscape is the unifying force, central to all the writing.

To gather their work I came to rely heavily on the knowledge and judgment of many people, among them Betty Rossi at Loonfeather Press in Bemidji; Anne Jenkins at the Minnesota Collection of the Duluth Public Library; Juanita Espinoza at the Native Arts Circle in Minneapolis; Mike McGinnis, Loree Miltich, and Tim Larson at Itasca Community College in Grand Rapids; Mary Bround Smith at Minnesota Literature in St. Paul; and Bonnie Kweik at the Minneapolis Public Library. I am grateful to them all.

My wife, Julie, was of great help, reading dozens of manuscripts, editing copy, and keeping records. Special thanks are due Todd Orjala, my editor at the University of Minnesota Press, for diligent editorial work and for making the hard decisions.

NORTH FROM DULUTH

Postcards from Duluth

Barton Sutter

Dull and Out of It

I live in Duluth, and I've got reasons. Lake Superior is a big one. Twenty-three streams running through town are twenty-three more. The largest natural sandbar in the world is another. And I'm tickled to live in a city where bears wander the streets every fall like country cousins come to town to see the sights.

Duluth has its cultural attractions, too—everything from a symphony orchestra to one of the best Greek restaurants in Minnesota. And yet I have the impression that many people, if they think of this city at all, consider Duluth a cold kind of joke, a Peoria of the North, the last outpost on the northernmost edge of the middle of nowhere.

One night last summer I was discussing this view of Duluth with my friend Roger, who moved here twenty years ago. "It's true," Roger grinned. "My relatives back in Kentucky still think of Duluth as a military base, some sort of radar station. They think we all live in Quonsets." We laughed and turned to watch a foreign freighter float off through the moonlight on Lake Superior. So

I would add to all the other pleasures of this place the sweet and luxurious feeling of being underestimated and misunderstood.

Lots of Duluthians, I've discovered, actually glory in this image of backwardness and do all they can to promote it, hoping, perhaps, to keep the hordes of tourists at bay. It's not unusual for natives to bad-mouth this town to outsiders, though I've noticed that the talk about terrible winters is often delivered with a sly smile. A few years ago the city put out bumper stickers that declared "We're Duluth and proud of it." I saw several that were customized to read "We're Dull and out of it." Obviously, Duluthians enjoy being out of the swim. And that's not just a metaphor. Lake Superior, the city's main attraction, remains too frigid for swimming for all but a couple of weeks of the year.

Duluth is hardly the little town that time forgot. This is a city of a hundred thousand odd souls, and some of them are lost. As in any other urban area in America, crooked politics, murder, racism, and rape are all committed here. So it's impossible to get too dewy-eyed about this place.

But there are pleasures to be had in a city like Duluth—and in Peoria, too, I imagine—that are unavailable to the residents of fancier towns. Among the most relaxing of these pleasures is the confidence that comes from knowing what you're not. Driving down Superior Street on a Saturday night in January, the sidewalks deserted, wind off the lake blowing snow through the pink light from the street lamps, the temperature stuck at twenty below, you know this isn't Paris. This isn't even Minneapolis. This is Duluth. You feel the truth of that.

Consequently, you can forget about the latest trends and fashions. No need to worry, up here, about which brand of mustard is "in." You can get by with jeans and a flannel shirt in even the snazziest restaurant. In that regard, life in Duluth is a great relief. And if lack of style sometimes amounts to a kind of pugnacious style itself, it's one that, personally, I find awfully appealing. I'm Duluth and proud of it. I'm Dull and out of it.

The Bridge

I'm pleased to announce that the Duluth Aerial Lift Bridge is once again in operation. As long as Lake Superior is locked with ice, there's no reason to raise the span, so for three long months each year, the Lift Bridge stands unmoving on the frozen lakeshore like a giant metal sculpture. But a few weeks back, the bridge began to lift to let the ships and ore boats slip through the canal again. Here on the northern edge of the known universe, robins are unreliable, tulips freeze overnight, and April showers turn to snow more often than to flowers. But once the Lift Bridge begins to rise and fall, we know we're connected to the rest of the world by water again, and we can safely expect some sort of summer before too awfully long.

Bridges are to Duluth what skyscrapers are to New York. They define the place. We've got the Bong. We've got the Blatnik. We've got trestles and docks and piers. We've even got a road called Seven Bridges. But the queen of them all, without doubt, is the Aerial Lift Bridge. Neither the longest nor the highest bridge in town, the Lift is merely the oldest and the loveliest.

Modeled after a bridge in France, the Lift began life back in 1905 as the Aerial Ferry Bridge. A carriage suspended from a steel framework carried passengers back and forth across the ship canal that had been dug through Park Point some thirty years before. In 1929 the transfer car was replaced by a movable steel span, and the bridge became the literal gateway to the harbor that we know today.

Wonderfully old-fashioned, graceful, light, and airy, the Lift Bridge is a beauty to behold and, over the years, has come to serve as a symbol for the city. It's our unofficial logo, and we duplicate it shamelessly—on flyers and brochures, on key chains, coffee mugs, and placemats—as if to say: This Bridge R Us. And in some strange way, it is. Location has a lot to do with that. The bridge is a kind of crossroads. It functions not only as a gate between the harbor and Lake Superior but also as an entrance to Park Point, the longest freshwater sandbar in the world. What's more, Lake Avenue, which runs across the bridge, divides Duluth in half, east from west. So the Lift Bridge stands at the center of the city, a sort of *X* that marks the most important spot in town.

I drove down to the bridge the other day and hit it lucky. A Canadian steamship was just heading out of the harbor, so I got to watch the span go up as the concrete counterweights, as large as cars, came down, and the big black boat, impressive as a grand hotel, trailing a veil of smoke from her stack, eased beneath the bridge and out to sea.

That was a sight, for sure, but this visit reminded me there's as much to hear as to see down at the ship canal: the catcalls of gulls, the swash and smack of waves against the piers, and then, as the boat approaches, the low, hoarse groan of her horn—long, short, short—and immediately, the higher-pitched response from the pilot house of the bridge—long, short, short. These horns are magnificent, really loud, even somewhat frightening. But there's also the trill of the bell that warns pedestrians to clear the bridge. And finally, once the span descends and traffic resumes, the hum of rubber tires on the metal grating of the roadbed. This rich texture of sound is so suggestive it can drive people slightly batty. My brother, a musician, spent an hour listening to the bridge one foggy night and came away with the lunatic desire to compose an orchestral piece called *Suite for Male Chorus, Triangle, and Aerial Lift Bridge*—a daringly innovative work that, I am sorry to report, remains unwritten at this date.

The awful truth Duluthians refuse to face is that the Lift Bridge is a preposterous anachronism. During the shipping season, Park Point residents get held up repeatedly by marine traffic passing through the ship canal. Cars back up and tempers rise right along with the roadbed of the bridge. This situation has spawned a verb that may well be unique to the city of Duluth. To be "bridged" means to be delayed by the rise of an aerial lift bridge, as in "Sorry

I'm late. I left the house at eight, but I got bridged." Any structure so troublesome that it causes alterations in the English language ought to be replaced by something more efficient—something large, concrete, and ugly. But I feel confident Duluthians would burn the mayor's house and drown him in the ship canal before they'd let that happen. For this old latticework of steel and sky is as important to Duluth as the Eiffel Tower is to Paris. The affection that city residents demonstrate for this impractical piece of architecture gives me great hope. It could be an early sign of true culture here on the northern rim of noplace in particular. And if we can feel affection and respect for a *bridge*—who knows?—someday we might even feel as much for nature or, impossible as it might seem, each other.

A Citty upon a Hill

In 1630, bound for Massachusetts Bay, John Winthrop preached a sermon in which he declared to his fellow Puritans, "Wee shall be as a Citty upon a Hill." And some politician in every damn American election ever since has felt compelled to quote him. Just you wait. Before this year is out, one of the presidential contenders is sure to tell the nation we ought to be a city on a hill. If we put that proposal into action, it would generate a lot of jobs—especially in the flatlands of Kansas and Nebraska—but of course our candidate won't mean for us to actually crank up the dozers and start moving dirt. No, he'll just be talking, as politicians will, meaning to imply that the U.S.—us—we ought to set some sort of spiritual and moral example for the world. But I don't trust this tired metaphor. Here in Duluth, we are not just *as* a Citty upon a Hill, we *are* a Citty upon a Hill, and a Citty upon a Hill has its downside, let me tell you.

Oh, the view is absolutely stupendous, no doubt about that. When my parents first brought me here as a kid, and Lake Superior opened out in front of me like an ocean, I lost my breath. I haven't quite got it back yet. Still today, when I drive in from the south, and the freeway lifts me over Thompson Hill, I hyperventilate. The hills of Duluth mark the beginning of the most crinkly country in Minnesota. Cartographers call these ups and downs *relief,* and that's what I feel whenever I return to Duluth, *relief* at having escaped the monotony of the plains that dominate most of the state. Whenever I feel cramped by daily duties, I can take a quick trip along Skyline Parkway, the road that rides the ridgeline for twenty miles through town. Or I can visit my pal Steve Pokorney, who owns a cheap little hilltop house and about the best view in all of Duluth. His house is far from fancy, but Steve can stand on his front stoop, the pauper prince of all he surveys, and observe the lower reaches of the St. Louis River, watch the tugboats nudge a freighter through the harbor, mark the long blue line of Minnesota's North Shore, look away to the green hills of Wisconsin, and try, at the far, hazy edge of the world, to separate sky from sweetwater sea. The view from this great hump of granite and basalt is downright thrilling, even spiritually uplifting, but I can't say I've seen much evidence that Duluthians derive any real moral benefit from living on a hill.

The one virtue Duluthians possess to a larger degree than other citizens of Minnesota—a state in which caution is a byword anyway, a state whose official motto ought to be "We'll see"—the one virtue on which Duluthians have an absolute lock is prudence. Natives are taught from birth to set the emergency brake and turn their wheels to the curb. Duluthians also know there are certain things you simply do not do. You don't mess with the winding streets of Little Italy in a blizzard. You don't go near Goat Hill all winter. And unless you're really, really bored, you don't turn down Nineteenth Avenue East in a sleet storm. Visitors take one look at Lake Avenue, which we used for a downhill ski race a couple years back, and wonder out loud how we drive this town in winter. I tell you, there's a weird satisfaction in seeing that the very streets of your city strike terror in a stranger's heart. But our secret is relatively simple: we stay home a lot. My grandparents, who spent most of their lives in West Duluth, had some very good friends who lived on the Heights. In order to visit them, my grandparents had to drive up Piedmont Avenue, which used to have a rope strung along the sidewalk so pedestrians could haul themselves uphill. "In winter," my grandmother explained, "we never saw those people."

Now, I believe in caution. I'm Scandinavian, after all, and I choose to live in this lopsided town where we've perfected the Minnesota Shuffle—that babystep technique that keeps you from knockin' your noggin on the ice. But prudence, the only virtue at which we actually excel in this particular city on a hill, strikes me as an awfully odd rallying cry. It's sort of boring, isn't it? And prudence has a dark side, too, as we're highly aware up here where ambition tends to be stymied by our belief that life is precarious and everything is going downhill. So the next time you hear a politician say we ought to be a city on a hill, ask him if he's ever been one. Better yet, offer him a ticket to Duluth. We like tourists, and we're served by a major airline—whenever the weather permits.

God

Having lived for several years beside "the shining big sea water," I've decided Lake Superior is God. Does that seem blasphemous? Any human view of God is bound to be imperfect, but, the way I see it, the image of Lake Superior is a lot less insulting to the Supreme Being than the more conventional picture of a graybeard in bathrobe and sandals.

If I remember right, Anselm was the saint who defined God as "that being than which no greater can be conceived." Well, I can't conceive of any being greater than Lake Superior. The ocean, sky, sun, the northern lights, the Milky Way—these are plenty great enough, but, to my mind anyway, they're all too distant and amorphous to truly qualify as beings. I saw a mountain in Norway once that seemed pretty great. I looked out the window of the train, and here was this tremendous . . . *being*. That great white rocky mountain looked alive; it seemed to pulsate, as if it had a heart; it spoke to me, and this is what the mountain said: "I am big, and you are very small." That mountain was probably God, but I only saw it once, and that was long ago and far away. We need our gods nearby. The ancient Greeks knew that. I live less than a mile from the greatest of all the great lakes, which is, for me, "that being than which no greater can be conceived."

To tell the truth, I've lived most of my adult life as a fairly arrogant agnostic. The existence of God seemed to depend on the mood I was in. If things were going badly, then there was no God, and, besides, He was a gigantic Jerk. If things were to my liking, my inner world felt a lot like Johnny Mathis singing "Misty," and I thought maybe God was everywhere but just invisible, like oxygen or something. I might have gone on, more or less content with my childish theology, except that I discovered, in the middle of my life, that such vague attitudes were harmful to my health. Apparently I'm like a Russian peasant; I have to have an icon. Without a clear image of God, my free-floating spiritual desire is apt to attach itself to the wrong object. I mean, I'm completely capable of thinking beer is God. Or sex is God. Or money. Or, hey, maybe I'm God! The world is full of dumb ideas, and half of them pass through my head each day. In order to protect myself from the more dangerous ones, I've decided Lake Superior is God.

I didn't come to this decision overnight. A quarter of a century ago, when I was in my early teens, my family stopped one evening in Duluth, and I ran down to skip rocks off the silver surface of Superior, to watch the water darken and go black. Gazing out over that great body of water, dizzied by the incense of spruce and balm of Gilead, I had what the psychologists call "an oceanic experience." This might be described as a semimystical state in which time slows down to zero and the boundaries of the self dissolve. To put it very poorly, I felt one with the universe. I felt grief, relief, melancholy, peace, and excitement all at once. Whatever that experience was in fact, it felt religious, and Lake Superior has been sacred to me ever since. Before I got married, I took a week and made a solo drive all the way around the lake. And ten years later, in the agony of separation and divorce, I drove down to the lake in desperation several times a day for days on end, as if that great sweetwater sea could heal me. And it did. Or nearly.

But I didn't know that I considered Lake Superior God until a couple years ago. One of the many pleasures of living in Duluth is that you have to look at the lake a lot. You might only mean to get some groceries or a hammer from the hardware store, but on your way you see something so grand, so terrible and beautiful, that you absorb your daily requirement of humility just by driving down the street. I've also found that the sight of Lake Superior works very well to shock me out of self-pity, a state of mindlessness to which I seem to be especially prone. I was deep in such a funk the night I finally realized that the lake was God.

I was driving home from the local shopping mall, where, once again, life had failed to fulfill my fantasies. Malls are all I need to know of hell, but I had eagerly agreed to go to hell because I had recently published a book, a book that represented my best efforts on this earth. So for two gruesome hours I had sat in a generic bookstore, like a kid at a Kool-Aid stand, smiling nicely at hundreds of people who looked right through me. I had sold and signed one book. Sick with shame, muttering murderous ideas, I topped the hill above the city and saw, straight ahead, the biggest, most gorgeous moon I'd ever witnessed in my life and there, below it, royal purple glinting gold from here to the edge of the world, Lake Superior. Only I didn't say, "Lake Superior!" I didn't say, "What a view!" I didn't say, "How beautiful!" No, no, no. Immediately, instinctively, I gave the lake its proper name. What I said was, "God!"

Tischer Creek

The other day I went out to see if Tischer Creek was still there after the long, harsh winter. Well, it was, thank goodness. The creek was up and running hard, burbling and yakking and rushing headlong down the dozens of waterfalls, large and small, that decorate its length as it drops toward Lake Superior. The sky was blue, the sun was warm, and the air was spiced with the incense of balsam and pine. After loitering along the creek for an hour, I could head back to the office, reassured that the world was still in working order.

Tischer Creek is one of my favorite places in all of Duluth. Twenty-three streams run down through this town to the lake—that's about one every mile—but Tischer is the one I think of as mine. That's odd. I live right next to Chester Creek, which is bigger and far more dramatic. There's a place on Chester Creek where, almost any summer day, you can watch brave boys, driven mad by sunshine and testosterone, leap off a thirty-foot bluff into a plunge pool below. That's always fun. And I love the Lester River, dark and sweet-scented, with broad, black pools, where I caught so many rainbow trout the first year I moved here. But Tischer Creek remains my favorite.

"Nature loves to hide," said Emerson, and it may be that I'm so fond of Tischer Creek because it's half-hidden and often overlooked. A wooden sign up from the bridge on Superior Street is the only hint the city offers, and that's pretty easy to miss. The tourists are all preoccupied with Lake Superior, which is pretty hard to miss, and Duluthians have so many other attractions to choose from that most days when I walk along Tischer Creek I get the whole ravine to myself.

A road runs alongside the creek, but it's blocked by a padlocked gate. I park the car beneath a big white pine and step out into the sound of the stream, which is like wind through the trees or waves breaking up on a beach, only different. This white noise is both varied and constant, and I will live in it until I leave the creek. The land that borders the creek, three quarters of a mile from Superior Street to Vermillion Road, was donated by Chester Congdon in 1908, and the city—out of laziness or wisdom (sometimes they're the same)—the city has done precious little to improve it. How can you improve what's perfect? A gravel hiking trail parallels the creek about thirty feet back from the water. Otherwise, the place is just itself, a miniature wilderness smack in the middle of the city.

Modesty, I've come to see, is part of Tischer Creek's appeal. Living in Duluth, you get to look at Lake Superior every day; the long view gives perspective and opens the mind. But Tischer Creek is intimate, encouraging those reveries that panoramas tend to wipe away. Here and there, the water widens into pools, but generally it looks as if a good broad jump would carry you across. The creek has all the features of a wild river—rapids, kettles, cataracts—it's just that they're small-scale.

If the place itself is modest, so are my expectations. I don't come here looking to see a moose. The wildest animal I've ever encountered in this ravine is a crabby red squirrel. I might see a sharp-shinned hawk shoot through the trees, but that would be exceptional. Normally, I have to be satisfied with watching water striders do their tricks and witnessing the tiny flowers for which I have no names. This morning, I'm surprised by a lowly toad, bumping slowly along the trail like a living lump of mud. I'm told there are brook trout in Tischer Creek, but I've never seen more than a minnow, and I've never bothered to bring a rod. Why should I? I don't want a thing out of Tischer Creek, not a fish, not a stone. It's just that every once in a while I need to be here.

The bedrock at the lower end of Tischer Creek, where I begin my walk, is feldspar—a soft, volcanic rock the creek has cut through like a liquid saw. Because this rock resembles human flesh, ranging in color from pink to red, the ravine always feels rather eerie here. As I move along the trail, I turn aside from time to time on paths that go right to the edge of the stream. People have just naturally worn these paths to their favorite sites along the creek. These places are like stations of the cross for pagans, and I pause at most of them. Here, for instance, I can step out on a little bluff beneath some big red pines and watch whitewater come rocketing down a redrock sluice and turn dark in the pool at my feet. There the foam on the surface swirls round in a pattern as attractive as the marbled endpapers you find in old, expensive books.

When I cross over Fourth Street, the bedrock turns black, a heavier, harder form of lava than the feldspar downstream. There are even more rapids and falls up here. And here's an especially sweet spot where I just have to stop and sit for a while. A big old willow leans over the stream, and its lines are so pleasing it looks like a kind of calligraphy. How the eye loves to follow a curve or zigzag. How interesting this crooked creek compared to any drainage ditch. Here water slips over a slanting ledge, pools, and cuts back the other way like a lesson in composition. Below the willow, beside the ledge, the mosses grow, both green and red. Here is the place, I tell myself, to bring your troubled mind. Here is the very place, I think, to just quit thinking altogether, watch the stream go by but stay but rush right past but still remain, giving off a sound like thunder, rain, and tiny bells.

When I hit Vermillion Road, I turn and hurry back down the trail, ignoring those places where I lingered before. I'm running out of time, and I've saved the best for last. Instead of heading up to the car, I leave the main trail and follow a rocky path right beside the creek until the ravine becomes a canyon with walls a hundred feet high. I'm lost in shadows now but come round a bend, and there's a surprise—a footbridge with railings, arching over the stream, as if it had grown right out of the rock. And further downstream there's another, and another—three bridges altogether, like reflections of each other. When I cross the last bridge, I'm standing on the canyon floor. I know I'm in Duluth, but I feel I'm somewhere else—Montana or Japan. The floor of the canyon is an alluvial fan of fine brown sand. I rest in the shade of a grand old willow while the creek curves away and flashes in the sun before it disappears in a tangle of brush. I visited Tischer Creek a half dozen times before I discovered her deepest secret. This is a place apart down here. The canyon has a mythic atmosphere. It's easy to imagine how a people might have made this womblike space their tribal source, the center of the earth from which the original folk went forth. Pleased to be here, I gaze up and up at the raw red walls, which are hung with cedars and little waterfalls that shatter in the sunlight.

As I climb up from the canyon to the car, I realize Tischer Creek has helped me see the difference between the things I think I want and what I really need, a distinction that seems to grow more crucial as we age. I'm absolutely crazy, for example, about the northern landscape. I'd like to buy the Boundary Waters. I'd like to own Alaska and kick everybody out except a couple friends. That's what I want. That's the size of my desire. But what I really need is to visit Tischer Creek now and again. I've read about a place in Russia where, every year, the locals contemplate certain sacred icons with such intensity that they are able to walk barefoot right through fire. Tischer Creek does something similar for me. I come here, not to think, but to wash away my worries, to rid myself of all my best ideas and fill up instead on images—dew in the grass, a bug on the water, sunshine on red rock—things that will sustain me when I go back to the world of cinder block and fluorescent lights where most of us work these days. Stuck with high tech ugliness, I listen for the shush and whisper of a stream called Tischer Creek.

At the Edge of Town: Duluth, Minn.

Carol Bly

Like all curmudgeons I am devoted to insulting someone's emotion of a given moment in hopes they will move away from it to a
germane but more ethical emotion. For example, curmudgeons
know that patriotism and nostalgia are the cheapest emotions
there are: bullies, especially, are much given to patriotism and nostalgia. Their eyes fill as Jimmy Stewart keeps Bedford Falls from
turning into Pottersville. Their eyes fill when someone drags out
the old Brownie 620 snapshots—but the weeper may in the very
next hour batter his wife or work out a new legal loophole for his
firm, giving it an extension on its wrecking the planet for profit. It
is not uncommon for lobbyists who contrive exquisite ways to
cheat the poor to have by heart several of Lincoln's bons mots. We
curmudgeons don't trust people who swing into a throaty tenor to
"Ich hatt' einen Kamerad." Teary memories are easy. Planning for
peace, difficult. Curmudgeons fear people whose hearts cry about
the past. Incidentally, a thoroughgoing nostalgia addict doesn't
stop at crying over lost wilderness in Brazil or Minnesota: he or
she mews over the manufactured U.C. British 1910s of *Master-*

piece Theatre, or the 1850s of the Dakotas, without knowing beans about either.

Patriotism is known as "the last refuge of the scoundrel," and nostalgia is one of the first demons psychotherapists relieve their clients of. But there is a third facile emotion: it is the virtuous feeling attendant upon loving natural places. People who feel it is actually *virtuous*, somehow, to love a place save themselves the pain of realizing there aren't many lovable places left. We curmudgeons worry, and then scold. We feel a sort of dread that so few people follow Wendell Berry from simple love of a particular countryside to thinking through *how* all systems connect, so we can try specific ways of amending our greed in order to preserve the patterns. For every person willing to do such thinking, there seem to be thousands simply feeling virtuous because they prefer woods to hotels or, say, Duluth's Lester Park Road to New York's Alphabets. They need to admit it takes money to live in beauty.

Money. The poor do not have the money of Kenneth Fearing or Louis Bromfield or Aldo Leopold or of the hundreds of people scribing logs and raising their cabins at the edges of forests. The "simple" life is a luxury. Second, nature lovers should figure out exactly who—which large groups—are ruining our planet. Then they should design conversations to have with high-up people in those organizations that would help those people identify finer feelings than conventional profit making.

Before going further, I would like to offer information that may surprise people who don't particularly cotton to the social-science approaches to ecology. In Minneapolis, the course at Central High School with the longest sign-up list is a new "interpersonal skills" course. Apparently, young people want to know how to talk to opponents so they won't feel hopeless. We lovers of place want to stop feeling hopeless, too. The social-work idea and the family-therapy idea is this: certain types of conversations serve to wake the torpid ethics even of administrators of rich organizations now wrecking human and animal and plant life. Sometimes, those people—very high-up, thoroughly middle-aged people—*change*.

A place lover of worth, then, is not a sixty-year-old noting how beautifully Duluth droops on its gigantic escarpment over Lake Superior. It is true that the foghorn's cold grunt, every three minutes of a thick summer morning, and the rocky edge and the mindless, beautiful forests running away northward, and the wind slaking down from Hudson Bay are wonderful—but a place lover of worth can't settle for rejoicing but must say, "Such love of place is simple. Anyone can hide in mere love of place. What is *uncomfortable* is to realize that the very rich are going to mine gold from northern Minnesota, splatting cyanide into the ground, because cyanide is a chemical used in the cleaning of gold from its coarse ore. The rich are going to sell the ancient forests of Canada (to Japan, of course, but not only to Japan), and for all the talk of reseeding, those forests will not regrow nearly so fast as they are taken."

It is so painful to think of all that the rich get away with. It is easier to rail at how the middle class manage their small holdings at the forest's edge. On the outlying roads of Duluth, for example—Arrowhead Road, Pike Lake Road, the Howard Gnesen Road—likely at the edges of anywhere, gravel driveways are flung down at short intervals across the raw culverts like little drawbridges to castles. The houses stand thirty or forty feet behind the ditchline, with pickups (while they still run) parked next to the kitchen door, and pickups (when they no longer work, and no one has picked up on the Coast-To-Coast FOR SALE signs in their windows) relegated to anywhere they will fit between the birches or Norway pines behind the house. To save a lot of money, you don't subscribe to the garbage service: you simply dump metal and glass trash farther back into the woods. You can play your rock all you like because this is the *edge,* not the center, of civilized life. There is more vandalizing of allotment gardens and toolsheds than there was during the 1930s, but there is no more disrespect for forest as such than there was then. As a child I grieved at any new building on these wild roads. It was as if the new little houses in their rows were dozens of little fists stuck into nature. Like all children who know some woods, I wanted the world to stay wild. Wild, to me and to my best friend, Arlene, was holy: city was dreamless. At nine years old, Arlene and I shook hands: when we were old, at forty, we would leave our husbands and go to the North Woods and live until we died in a log cabin. Forty years later, I visited Arlene during the week before she died of cancer. I asked her when I should come. Nights, she said: would you come at two or three in the morning? Right. That was when the drugs didn't cover well. That was when her exhausted husband was asleep. It was hard to hover by her bed, dangling one arm on her tubings stand, watching as she gathered herself from the dispersal of pain in order to say a sentence. She was spooky with drugs, too. "We had better do it," she made out to me. "We had better do it—go to the log cabin in the North Woods." I said, "That was one of the best ideas you and I ever had."

When we love our planet so much, it seems queer that we haven't talked everybody into saving it. Perhaps what stands in our way is those very feelings of virtuousness that nature lovers indulge in. I have put together three likely reasons for their holierness-than-thou.

First, perhaps nature lovers lack compassion for those who live in ugly places because they don't *know* how ugly people have made the earth. Joan Didion recently remarked in the *New York Review of Books* that "what is singular about New York, and remains virtually incomprehensible to people who live in less rigidly organized parts of the country, is the minimal level of comfort and opportunity its citizens have come to accept."

Or second, perhaps we all make a virtue out of anything we enjoy lest we otherwise feel guilty that others haven't the same blessing. I have even heard men feel virtuous because they weren't bald. Surely the unconscious chooses that attitude so it won't have to feel sorry for people who are bald. If we noticed that others haven't the same access to land that we have, we would suppose we ought to share with them—but there are so *many* of them! And the poor often have not been brought up with a taste for quiet solitude, reading, listening to Mozart. If they came to our edge of wilderness they would hound loons, otters, and philosophers with TV-ad values—rock, loud motors for the skiers shouting "Hit it!" a thousand times in an afternoon, snowmobiles to shatter the snowy woods' quiet. It is education (alas) that makes people use nature quietly.

The third reason for virtuous feeling is that it is psychologically natural to regard nature as holy. It is a necessary part of stage development to ascribe *holiness* to what lies far outside our parents. Here is how this worked in me. My father was a very high-minded, fallen-away Presbyterian. Once he discovered that good churchmen were frequently just as crooked as nonchurchmen, he left the church. My mother came from a gregarious, confident family of agnostics, every one. Both parents either growled or joked about the Sunday school pamphlets I brought home. "Color Jesus's robe blue," went the instructions, and I had happily done so. "Color his hair yellow." (Of course! This was Minnesota in the 1930s!) "Leave his gown white. Lightly shade in brown and yellow together to make the sands of Judea." Sunday schools did not yet provide three-tiered Crayola boxes, which held so many colors we might have given a different blue each to the Sea of Galilee and the Jordan and the Red Sea. Both parents jeered at my pastel Jesus. Well—but kids are brave. I tried again: I recited for them my Memory Line: "The Lord God loves each one of us like a child." No god in his right mind, my mother allowed, would love our species with its hypocrisy, its warmongering, and its racism. We were a family where Mussolini's cruelty in Abyssinia got discussed at the table. There were often quite crispy phrases floating about our living room, such as God would be an idiot to love our species and therefore, since God is not an idiot, there is no God, all said with a lift of the chin.

That is all very well for *adults*, but a psychological fact is that if *children* are locked out of feeling loved by the gods of Duluth churches, they will go looking for a god they *can* imagine and feel loved by. It is a healthy wanting for a species with a neocortex, after all: we have to move away past our parents to what is greater, more general—the *omnium invisibilium*. As species go, the human one is partial to concepts. We love to connect unlike things by metaphor, and once we've got the taste for it, we are never satisfied with just the actual parents anymore.

So when conventional religious adoration is not allowed, the child turns pantheist, if that child has any access at all to natural landscape. I gratefully pottered about the rough paths of Hunter's Hill, the rock outbreaks between the Jean Duluth Road and the cliff edge, and, with Arlene, who had a satisfying penchant for the morbid, fantasized about all the dead at the bottom of Lake Superior. Virginia Woolf said we must each live in the world of people and the world of trees: I went 87 percent for trees. As I played in the vacant dairy pastures, I was sorry each time a new road was cut through to the forest.

It has been over a century since Tolstoy remarked (in the first paragraph of the novel *Resurrection*) that adults concentrate so hard on pushing coal smoke and naphtha into the sky—and cheating one another—that they fail to enjoy this world given to us for our joy. There is some good to shaming, which Tolstoy intended with that passage, but not enough. Corporations still mine and wreck the environment. Perhaps we people who so much love certain *places* and who know there is a "sense of place" that can exhilarate the mind need to think of ourselves as corporate shareholders. If we do not own stock in companies ourselves, perhaps we know relations or friends who do. At least we can imagine ourselves to be shareholders. What if we were Exxon shareholders? It is likely that thousands of us would gladly have eschewed 0.3 percent of our dividend (if that's what it would have taken) to fire a drunken captain or to mount job searches for sober captains. Corporations lie a good deal. Perhaps they lie in saying that all their shareholders want is profit. Perhaps the fee owners of mining companies do not want cyanide trickling or splashing into the aquifers of northern Minnesota. If keen businesspeople in fact have better ethical instincts than their groups claim they have, we need a new kind of conversation—the kind called group consciousness raising.

Growing up on the line between two opposites—town and wilderness—has disabused me of any notion that opposed ideas make restful tangents. But I have also stood on the line between literature and social psychology. Literary people look down on social psychologists and usually refuse to see how they can change attitudes in fairly rigid, grown-up people. Social scientists are more and more using literature in their training programs, but what they respect least in literati is the puling nature lover who neither in poetry nor in fiction takes on the big boys—those in extractive industries. Social scientists would like us writers to drop the vague sensitivity and learn skills like intentional interviewing—if we really want to save our place.

Let's give ourselves, right here, two minutes' jeering at phrases like "group consciousness raising" and "intentional interviewing." How revolting the jargon of the social sciences is! So turgid is it, in fact, that for every Ernest Becker and Virginia Satyr and Murray Bowen there seem to be hundreds of social workers and therapists whose prose is so abstract, given to generalities, and without particulars that their own colleagues refuse to breast through the sludge of it.

But when we are done insulting their bad writing, let's tell the social scientists that we want to learn their jargon (for its accuracy) and their new processes. Put simply, it is the therapists and social workers and group psychologists who can move a polluter from his or her laugh, "Yeah? Just try fighting profit and progress, chump!" to noticing that some part of that very polluter really doesn't want to wreck the Arctic, or the Antarctic, or the places between that we love.

We had better approach the rich shareholders or extractive industries than settle for snapping at small-scale trashers and polluters on near-the-city roads. Besides, a couple of hours a month studying how actually to *change* planet-wrecking organizations will be such horrible work we can feel conscientious about it. If we did two or three *days'* worth of learning this new field—intentional interviewing—even the crossest of us curmudgeons could relax as we regard Duluth's choppy harbor—or any harbor. For we would know we had done very modern, very exacting, intelligent labor for our planet. We could relax as we hike lightly between (not on) lichen and flowers of St. Louis County—or of any county.

Breaking the Ribbon
Roger K. Blakely

Lake Superior to the south, woods and bluffs to landward compress society along Highway 61 into a monofilament. A break in the thread of its beadlike towns (as happened when cloudbursts washed out the Caribou Bridge a few years back) maroons people for days, except for untrustworthy backcountry roads.

So human contacts acquire a scarcity value. Most of the resort owners fraternize; their rivalries defer to their common financial interests. Truckers, mail carriers, school buses deliver precious gossip as a second payload. The speed of traffic, the instantaneity of Duluth TV (snowy without good aerials), the basketball tournaments, 4-H, ice cream socials and bake sales and flea markets and art fairs relieve the loneliness somewhat.

Still, it's different here, especially off-season. Campers, house trailers, backpackers thin out then; only snowmobilers and skiers come, and the latter are a compulsive, unrooted species dashing from Lutsen slopes to Grand Marais bars and back again. The people who belong are Lindstroms, Helbergs, Becklunds, Nordholms, and other descendants of those first tillers and fishers and sawyers and storekeepers who rebuilt Scandinavia like a second Troy on this cold coast thousands of miles from their forebears' birth-beds and graves.

Although they follow Oprah and pro football like everyone else, these Olafsons and Berglands also observe Sittende Mai or Svend-skarnasdag; and on Lucia Day (December 13) the eldest daughter of a traditional Swede household wears a crown of lighted candles to serve her parents breakfast in bed of strong coffee, sweet rolls, and cookies pressed into the shape of cats. At least in the old days.

Finns likewise celebrate St. Urho's Day on March 16 in memory of the hero who chased the grasshoppers out of Finland. Some say he chased everyone who could read and write out of Finland—an interpretation disputed by loyalists.

These northerners of diverse nationalities are the people who know, and do, and deal cannily but honestly, and keep the dignity of the past. Their children and children's children have scattered; there are no roots for most of these offshoots on hardscrabble shores. Being bright, industrious, and bold, they attend college, take city jobs, go into business, buy and sell, visit home, phone home, look south and east, and find good or average luck there, expecting high civilization to erase the imprint of frosts, fogs, blizzards, and wolf-howls.

Some of them remain or return. Add to this indigenous core the visitors whose winterized summer cottages evolve into retirement homes close to the ski lifts and the lounges and the rockhound beaches and birds. If amenities are lacking and doctors scarce, thugs and muggings and foul air and noise and political scams are scarcer still. We value these small, secure northcoast refuges from a decaying America, and hope only that the right sort of people (who can define them?) gather here as a saving remnant.

Still, aliens feel the difference. Like the Caribou, some bridges are difficult to build or maintain. One remembers, for example, a random Sunday morning. In an unmowed field stands a church of board and battens, pitched roof, scrollwork belfry straddling a ridgepole. Worshipers in sober black or subdued prints come out the door. An ancient flower-hat bobs like a chalice. They start their cars or converse in pairs and quartets while the banality of "Softly and Tenderly" seeps from the nave. A wheezing organ stops in mid-phrase and its musician appears at a window to check the weather. Autos retreat single file. Pastor Jorgenson, if that's his name, in street clothes and a visor cap from a farm-implement company, shuts the door, rattles its knob, and shuffles crosslots toward a parsonage among birches. Our dawdling tourist wants Kodachromes of the church interior, but of course it's locked now. So he drives off too, wondering not altogether ironically what eternal pastures await this flock. Wondering too where strays like himself congregate for lunch.

Or the same tourist descends a switchback to the lake. Split Rock Lighthouse punctuates an upshore cliff. Hot, hazed sunlight makes the head throb; a stench of herring persists; the waves glow pewter, not azure, on a day when nature, to quote Emily Dickinson, is caught without her diadem. But a big, easygoing fellow in shorts, bare-chested, slouches Rodin-style on top of a boulder large as a refrigerator. His tripod supports a 4x5 Graphic with lens zeroed on the lighthouse's bigger optics. Obviously this outmoded Ansel Adams gear works wonders in expert hands.

The suntanned cameraman looks native or else assimilated. Calmly he lights a cigar from the stump of another. Calmly he opens a beer and offers his new audience its mate. Yes, he wants pictures but the light's not right. See those shadows in the wrong places?

The tourist nods sympathetically. They chat. The tourist finishes his Pabst and ponders the empty can. He hates to drop it in front of an initiate. The expert grins, catches it, tosses it into a duffel bag. True outdoorsmen tote out of the wilds any junk they carry in.

A day later our traveler's curiosity tempts him down the same path the same time of afternoon, and of course the photographer waits in identical pose, a few hours more suntanned, smoking a descendant of the first cigar. No, the light's still wrong, although it looks pristine to the other. The light's not right, but it will be, today or tomorrow or eventually, so what's the rush?

In principle the traveler agrees. In practice, he's due in St. Paul by suppertime.

Or there's the memory of a girl in dirndl and red windbreaker at roadside, her book bag and canvas luggage at her feet and a violin case under her arm, late on a Sunday. Either she missed the bus or buses don't run here. Without exactly hitchhiking, she signals willingness to ride—with qualified persons. Driving past with slow reflexes, you catch the lilt of her shoulders, the smile, the taffy hair and high cheeks of a Viking. Did she spring full grown from waves? Did this belle of the North graduate successively from hopscotch and tug-of-war and pajama parties and a crown of candles and baton twirling to a major in music at the university branch? Is she mortal, or the genius of the place?

Of course you back and turn at the next driveway to retrace your route and solve the mystery, but at her corner stands only an elaborately painted and carved Uncle Sam holding a mailbox in his two outstretched palms. She rode away with someone else, this lost princess of the imagination, while you temporized.

At Duluth, though, the lake surrenders to dry land, the ribbon breaks, a freeway arches topside to Minnesota plains, thunderheads steal the sun, and you discount those fancies of half an hour, half a destiny ago. But you never forget them.

The North Shore

Sheila Packa

Love: Highway 61, to the Canadian border, the east violently blue,
liquid, crashing on the water-worn ledge of rock, the west, rivers
dropping and pines growing deep on the hills and Sawtooth Mountains, and south, behind me like the past.

Memories: immigrant grandparents who stepped off trains onto
platforms made of raw lumber, into northern wilderness, to become farmers who harvested stones, tomatoes, cucumbers. They
salted and smoked their trout, whitefish, herring. They boiled coffee with an egg in the pot in their tiny frame houses impaled on
chimneys, the woodstove hot in the burning cold. The old-timers
talk about winters they've known, storms and shipwrecks, bridges
washing out, and thick fogs. Never love. Love can't be talked
about—it's too vast and too unpredictable.

Music plays back there in the past, always. The bellows of an ac-
cordion breathe. A grandfather or an uncle comes back. When I
think of them, I think of a saw and its long springy blade with tiny
sharp teeth and a worn wooden handle carved with fleur-de-lis.
After the trees were cut, they went to the mill to be sawn into

boards. The roar is deafening. The big circular saw blurs, the sharp mound of damp sawdust rises, and the sweet-smelling pine boards are stacked to dry. More memories rise: saunas on Saturday nights, dances. Bubbles rise in a glass of beer, golden with a white head of foam, my mother's dress sways in the night, a car door slams, tires roll on the gravel of the driveway, the red taillights disappear. I hear the wind.

The saw rusted. It hangs on the wall in my basement. Oil me, it says; use me.

On Sundays, when I was small, our family took the bridge between Duluth and Superior to visit my aunt. I peered just above the back door of the car to see the startling high horizon of the lake. The concrete columns of the bridge flew past as we rose higher and higher; suddenly the tires whirred over the iron bridge deck. The car slid under the grid of beams and then out into unbarred sunlight. Down into Wisconsin we drove, past grain elevators and a round fuel tank I thought was as big as the world itself. *Watch out,* my sister whispered, *it might roll right over us.*

My grandfather built a wooden horse. He carved the head and body, made both very smooth and joined them using a branch for a neck. He cut four pieces of a small tree for the legs, painted the horse black and white, fashioned a leather bridle and made the tail from frayed binder twine. The horse was wild. My father said you could always tell that about a horse if it has a blaze down its face. The horse threw me off; I skinned my knees but I got back on, riding until the joints swung back and forth. Then one day, my grandfather died. I tied the wooden horse to a red pine in the backyard.

I stayed home because my mother didn't believe that children should be taken to funerals. They buried him. In the yard, the legs of the wooden horse sunk into the sand. Using a phrase I'd heard, I said, *he's going down.* He's sinking.

When my father was young, in 1923, his father tucked the children into the seats of a horse-drawn sleigh to go to school. When the children were settled under the blanket, he slapped the horse's rump and it took off, driverless, toward the one-room school-house. In the school yard, the horse stopped and the children climbed down, then the horse took the sleigh back to my grandfather. Soon there were too many children for the sleigh, so my father's father built a long carriage, the first school bus in the area. Then he took the reins himself. After a while, my grandfather bought a Model T. He traded one of the plow horses for a gold watch. My grandmother got mad; there were mouths to feed. But he didn't stop. When he wanted to swap the farm in Zim (a small community near Hibbing) for some acreage in Sax, closer to the swamp, she told him to go ahead, without her. She kept the school bus contract and sold eggs, milk, and blueberries. She pounded wool into felt mittens and hats. He moved to a one-room shack, fifteen miles away.

He drank home brew. One night, he heard a noise at the door. "Who's there?" he shouted. There was no answer so he shouted again. He heard a board creak on the step, but still no answer. There was no window in the door, and none near it. It was late. My grandfather aimed his rifle and shot through the planks. He passed out. When the sun came up, he woke and drew the bolt. A bear lay dead at his feet.

Watch out who you marry, my mother said.

Watch out for bears, my father said.

In the summer, my father took me to watch bears at the dump. At dusk, the shadows began to take shape and climb the heaps of garbage. I clutched my father's arm with terror and excitement as the black animals sat and licked out the inside of cans and chewed up butcher paper. I dared not sit near the window nor go outside, no matter how urgently I needed to. Around us, the dump smoldered.

My father found a lot of treasure at the dump. He brought it home. When he left, my mother threw it away, again. She always tossed things with passion; she enjoyed it. "We aren't going to use this," she said, swinging a box—of what? papers, old irons, bent tools?—into a rusted barrel at the end of the driveway. According to her, we weren't going to use much of anything.

"You can always get by," she instructed me, but she acknowledged that it helped to have a certain amount of luck.

When the sky is overcast, Lake Superior turns the color of lead. The wind from the lake is stunningly cold. In the spring, when the smelt run, people dip their nets into the rivers and fill up buckets with the flashing fish. In the right time, in the right place. These fish are a delicacy. Cut off their heads, eviscerate them with sharp scissors, rinse until the water runs clear, dip into a beer batter, fry, and eat. Beer will help you swallow. A lot of beer helps you swallow anything.

Just so you aren't swept off your feet into dangerous currents. Just so you don't drown.

I nearly drowned in Lake Esquagama once. A girl saved me. My mother didn't know that I was swimming. In fact, I was at the place she had forbidden me to be in without her or my sister. I was seven and thought all I had to do to swim was to believe that I could swim. Believing, I went in over my head. The lake swallowed me, as I swallowed its golden red light. In a moment of panic, reality struck. The Bronzwyck girl lifted me up by my straps and set me back on the shore. I ran up the hill, south along the highway, back to my mother.

Another memory. My mother and I stand at the window in my grandmother's kitchen, at the sink. The hot water faucet doesn't work because there is no hot water; also, the sink has no plumbing. Water falls down the drain into the slop pail, which must be dumped outside before it overflows. We aren't bothered by any of this. The other window in the kitchen looks out onto the cold porch. My grandmother stores food out there, a roasted turkey and apple pies. On the top shelf in the kitchen cupboard is a bottle of brandy. My grandmother pours herself a shot, downs it with one swallow, and wipes her lips with the back of her hand. *Let her,* my mother said once, to one of her sisters. *Let her enjoy the peace of our father's death.*

Outside the window is the backyard, then the barn and barnyard. Beyond that is a field, the woods, and then the swamp. The swamp is where my mother said she hid from her father once when he was wildly drunk and seized the rifle and aimed it at the children. Shots rang out.

But that was a long time ago and he's dead. So is my grandmother and so is my mother. But not love. Love is never dead. It's been passed down like the love of music and the love of working with the hands. We inherit our tools. My two-year-old cousin loves his saw so much that he must sleep with it in his crib.

I used a saw to build a rabbit hutch. I nailed a little scrap of lumber on the frame to make a latch. I turned the latch around and around, charmed by its simplicity, its utility. The next morning when I went out to feed my rabbits, they were gone.

The old road. Highway 61 once had no tunnels. The road at Silver Cliff was slung on the steep slope over the lake; the road was narrow, like a rope. You could look down and down and not see a shore, only the high line of the watery horizon. It took the breath away; it could take your life.

So can love.

My first honeymoon trip was to Grand Marais. My husband at that time did not sightsee. Rather, he drove in a dogged fashion, worrying over a rattle in the dash of the car. He asked me to listen—*listen!*—to the noise instead of gazing at the birch trees in a blur along the road. Every now and then, the blue and silver light off the lake flashed at me. I ignored the rattle. Then the next evening, my husband cut his finger on a razor in the suitcase. "See what you did," he said, blaming me for the way I packed our things. He kicked me. I had never been kicked, my mother had never been kicked, and I don't think my grandmother had ever been kicked. The horizon rose in my mind, the feeling of being on a narrow road, like a rope. I heard the whir of an iron bridge deck, the barred sunlight, and saw that world. It was rolling over me, just like my sister had said. Waves rolled in my head, like breakers.

Five years later, in a hard rain, I was with a different man. He was to become my second husband. We drove along Highway 1, the long and winding road east of Ely to the North Shore. At the time, he was married to somebody else. It was slow going; the windshield wipers didn't work fast enough to keep our vision clear. The road had almost no shoulder, making it dangerous to stop. We slowed even more. Suddenly, we saw russet and black shadows, long oblongs, in the sweep of headlights along the ditch. Moose. Several moose, big ones and small ones. He steered carefully between them. Moose are unpredictable. They can take umbrage and charge, undaunted by a vehicle. We slipped past them and had dinner at a restaurant that served salad from a bed of chipped ice in a silver canoe.

I have heard that the lake has its illusions. Sometimes the vapor rising off the surface magnifies or distorts. Images can reverse themselves. A freighter, I've been told, can appear upside down. Love must be like this mist. The Anishinaabe tell stories of the lake, Manidoo, "mystery." Fishermen have stories. Women have stories. So many lives have slipped or surrendered.

At dinner that night, my future husband ate some bad fish. He became ill and stayed in the bathroom while I sipped wine, a whole bottle, and watched the indigo shimmer of night on the lake. Love is as vast and as unpredictable as Lake Superior. Yet I look to love. I look to the lake when I've lost my way, so I might find it again.

There have been wrecks; people and boats have never been found. Men have lost women in this sea, women have lost husbands. His wife was about to lose hers and I was losing my footing, I was in too deep. My marriage to him also failed.

Good luck, bad luck, how much has luck to do with love?

Almost anything my father fixed, he referred to as a "she." If it was an engine, she wouldn't run. If it was a radio, she wasn't picking up the signal. If it was a boulder to be moved from the yard, she was stubborn. All things in this way were temperamental and needed to be cajoled. The lake also is a she.

If you stand on certain places of the North Shore you stand on rock. Jutting granite plates crack and wear finally into tiny rounded pebbles that shift beneath your weight. If a stone can split, so can a marriage. If a seed can take root in stone, which happens over and over again on the bluffs, so can new love reach toward the sun even from the most unarable ground or the most intemperate climate.

That saw of my grandfather's . . . he used it. He cut down a large share of the forest. He felled and ripped virgin pines through his saws. All of this to make a house. The surface of each board is lined with grain, jagged until it is smoothed with a rasp. You can make anything you want; you can ply boards into a boat if you bend them with steam. Work with the hands, I learned. Measure carefully, then cut. Save what you can and reuse it. Burn what you have to. Give your full attention to these details. Work with, not against. Balance. See which way she wants to go.

My material is language, my material is love.

When I had a child, I brought him to the harbor in Duluth to watch the ships. The lakers, long freighters low in the water, carry ore in their holds, and other ships carry grain. Each enters the canal, coming and going, Greece, Portugal, Canada, Russia, Pittsburgh, come to the inmost shore while my son swims on Park Point, riding the wake of the ships.

The lake sorts things out: sand on the south beach, smooth rock on the west beach; each time a wave pulls back, I hear a clatter. Driftwood washes up to dry, silver. The shore carries the water's engravings. Another language. There have always been at least two languages around me, English and Finnish. One I knew and one I didn't know, like the language of the body and the language of the spirit. One physical and one beyond the capacity of my senses.

I am going north along the shore now, bringing my craft with me. A woman sits next to me, her hair auburn and gold and brown and silver, catching the light. Between Grand Marais and Grand Portage, along the line of trees, an owl flies.

This past winter, in the burning cold, ice shattered stones. After that the lake threw off the ice, heaped it up in huge drifts the color of pale jade. Then suddenly, the ice was gone. The water turned sapphire.

Love is the attention to detail.

Highway 61, to the border. The Monson truck that I passed has passed me. I share coffee with my friend. There is a perfect quay ahead but we aren't there yet. We're here, always, beneath the flash of hawk's wings, migrating. Fledging.

OUR PLACE IN THE WOODS

Where I Ought to Be

Marlon Davidson

The highest point on the property where I live is an old bare hill with some scrubby sumac and sere grasses. It is shaped like a great breast, and each time I look at it I am reminded that landscapes often look like the human figure in repose, nudes, sleeping giants, pregnant women. Do other people see these reclining figures in the shapes of the earth or do I look for them, manufacture them out of a lifetime of drawing the human figure, considering it, as I do, the ultimate work of the Creator? I do the same thing with cloud formations, just like Lucy in the *Peanuts* cartoon, who said she saw "The Stoning of Stephen" in a cumulous cloud. With Lucy as inspiration, we might write history or fiction by beginning with landscape.

To the north this hill overlooks small and shallow Goose Lake with its two dark wooded islands, hay fields beyond to the horizon. To the south, partially hidden from view, is the county road, known as the Powerdam Road, its blacktop flatness appearing three times between lower hills, the few passing cars too distant to hear. Both to the east and to the west are densely wooded areas, mixed deciduous hardwoods and a lot of mature poplars, all three types, balm of Gilead, a fragrant tree, the first to lose its leaves in fall soon after turning an amazing metallic gold. There are also many tall graceful quaking aspen and the big-toothed variety, a magnificent tree that can grow to enormous size, the trunk growing black and gnarled with age, even splitting open like an overripe and decaying fruit. Below the hill, at the end of a meandering path, is the grove of hundred-year-old white pines and only slightly younger Norways that surround the main house and garden areas. The landscape all around is a world within itself, my world, the place I know better than any other at this time of my life. I have walked over it all and deep into the woods. I know where the trillium and the yellow lady's slipper bloom and where the erotically shaped jack-in-the-pulpit grows. The view from the hill brings all these secrets to my mind and I feel like the master of a kingdom, though I know this is pure fantasy and that nobody really owns anything. And I know too that I could give it up and walk away from it without looking back, as I have done several times before. There is always another hill, another vista beyond it and other visions to be had, even in places beyond this island of peace, which seems to be home at this point in my life.

We have a bench at the top of the hill, a place to sit and look around; a place to meditate. My cat, Pedro, who always follows me when I walk, likes to stretch out there and allow the sun to warm his belly while he works his claws in and out, unashamedly ecstatic and sensual, acting out the phrase "as comfortable as a cat." His days are spent in a great deal of lazing, sleeping in the most comfortable places he can find, chasing after mice and red squirrels, eating, watching a butterfly, amazed, as if it were the first butterfly on earth, or the last, then sleeping again. An ideal life, it seems to me, and a sensible affront to the crazy behavior of humans, so preoccupied with their schedules and responsibilities. We could learn something from the animals and their unashamed acceptance of life as it is, of its gifts, its offerings, if we will only look around. My cat sends a line of poetry through my mind: "The world is too much with us; late and soon, getting and spending, we lay waste our powers." The bench at the top of my hill is a place to make sense out of things, to find, in a phrase that is deceptively simple but critical, what the really important things are. I tell my friends, "Find a hill. Go up there and sit and let your brain empty, wait for the message, because there will be a message. If you are open to it."

Why do we go to the hills? It seems that something pulls us there, some mysterious force. The prophets went to the mountain-tops to seek epiphany, to bring back down to earth the command-ments of God. The saints, the holy men and women of old were gathered up to glory from mountaintops. "I will lift up mine eyes unto the hills, from whence cometh my help," asserts the Psalmist, and how can it be said any better than that? Even so minor an elevation of land as my hill seems to draw me there when I feel a need for quietness and reflection. The distances are soothing to my vision and I realize how I need to see a horizon, like a string long and straight, uncluttering my mind.

Under the last full moon, I walked up there in the dark, just after moonrise, that orange orb standing over the dark trees like a great Oriental lantern. I sat on the wood bench, having left Pedro behind to torture, as cats will, the mouse he had just pulled out of the grass. I would contemplate the great philosophical problem of why cats will torture their prey instead of eating it, and beyond that the puzzle of the food chain and its cruelties. The lake lay in a long inky band, the islands now merely dark ominous forms, no light anyplace except for that melon-colored circle to the east. Suddenly, over my head, I heard the beating of wings, like a host of angry angels had come for me. I nearly jumped up and made for the path, counting my recent sins. But then I heard the first honk-ings and recognized the sound of the geese, their squawkings and yakkings as they beat their way down to the lake surface, passing directly over my head. I could almost feel the pulsing air from the beating of those powerful wings. They passed on into the darkness, but momentarily I heard the numerous splashings of their landings. There were many birds. I counted the landings but lost track. Then there was the loud chatter of their happy arrival, the conversation of partners who mate for life. Behind me in the dense wood, an owl spoke a question. I thought of Isak Dinesen and a passage from her book *Out of Africa,* one I often say to myself when I accept one of nature's gifts, just as she did on another hill in Kenya: "Here I am where I ought to be."

From the Rio Grande to the Rainy

Bobbie Greiner

A gusty northwest breeze nudges my body as I slowly ascend a nearly vertical ladder. I pause to catch my breath and glance up up toward my goal, a Minnesota Department of Natural Resources cupola sitting atop this sixty-five-foot fire tower frame like an eagle's nest at the top of a tall, thin spruce. It is the first week in May of 1994, fifty-nine degrees—bright, sunny, windy. The as yet leafless popple, birch, and maple surrounding my tower sway in the breeze like long slough grass in rippling water.

Migrating juncos—plump, satiny gray ground-feeding birds—forage over the forest floor the way cattle graze a pasture. But unlike fenced, domesticated animals, the juncos are only passing through. These small flocks appear briefly every spring and fall as, instinctively, they travel north for the summer and south for the winter. A dozen or so birds below me scratch and pick, rustling across last year's wind- and sun-dried leaves even as the wind sighs through the treetops.

It's a cold wind, a transitional, between-the-seasons wind whose winter bite is mediated only by the spring sun's warmth. And, like the birds and the wind, these northern woodlands are also in transition. Winter's snow cover is gone. Summer's fire-retardant-green leaves will not appear for another six to eight weeks. The woods stand naked and defenseless, especially vulnerable to fire. Fires set by people burning last year's dead growth from fields and yards; fires that tend to get away from those who set them—which is why I am here right now. This is my job.

For several weeks during northern Minnesota's spring fire season, my husband and I work for the DNR office located in Birchdale, our small community straddling Highway 11 between International Falls and Baudette. Jim is a "smoke chaser," one of those on the ground who battle fire with hand tools and five-gallon pump cans (pee cans, more informally) strapped to their backs. As Birchdale's official tower lookout, I battle fire from my lofty perch with binoculars and a plot map as my tools.

Now above the swaying treetops, I catch a whiff of springtime fragrance and I stop again, suddenly aware of just how much these elements of my world please me: the smells, the birds, the trees. In the way the sun heats my body, my inner person is warmed by the landscape before me—Koochiching County in northern Minnesota, the place I now call home.

I've lived in northern Minnesota nine years, yet I am only beginning to understand what people mean when they talk about going home; about the urge to return to one's birthplace; about how the landscape molds a person as surely as does the nurturing, or the neglect, of mother and father.

This sense of belonging to, and identifying with, a particular spot on earth is something for which I have spent my life searching.

My journey began fifty-one years ago when I was born in Brownsville, Texas, a community situated on the north bank of the Rio Grande and our country's southernmost border with Mexico. My nomadic childhood and youth were spent moving between

Texas, Colorado, and Washington State. From my late teens until my early forties, I lived in California, both northern and southern. At forty my search took me to the wilds of Canada's Yukon Territory.

The Yukon's rugged beauty was my idea of heaven on earth. I wanted to stay there for the rest of my life. But circumstances intervened, and I returned to California, my life as unsettled as always. Three months later I met Jim, with whom I moved to Minnesota.

As I think back, I see myself as having been a wind-borne seed, similar to those that float past my fire-tower windows on these spring days. Like the seeds whose movements are dictated by the shifting wind, my thoughts drift between past and present, and I can't help but marvel at the ways fate led me to this place.

For I was an urban child, a lonely, redheaded, freckle-faced little girl with her nose pressed against the windows of intangible city walls. As a prison inmate dreams of escape, I gazed outward and wished to walk in the shelter of tall trees, to wade in cool creek water, to breathe clean air. I wanted to live in the places I could only read about in books and over whose photos I pored in the glossy pages of *National Geographic* magazines. To me, those distant valleys, meadows, and forests symbolized the good life. If I could only get "out there," I knew my life would be different.

But I was imprisoned by circumstances beyond my control. Both my parents, who divorced before I was five, were heavy drinkers, alcoholics with neither the interest nor the funds to invest in land— or in children. I grew up in the wilderness environment of the bars and alleys of the many cities in which we lived. I knew the streets the way my neighbors know the woods and rivers of their homes in northern Koochiching.

When I was a child, my mother moved my younger brother and me often, outrunning bad checks, abusive boyfriends, and her own guilty conscience. When I grew old enough to do my own packing, I stored my cardboard boxes under my bed or in a closet, because I knew I would be needing them. When times were especially shaky, I didn't unpack at all, but lived out of my shabby luggage the way world-class travelers live out of leather suitcases. I became so used to moving that it no longer hurt to leave friends. I had so few.

Barely eighteen, I married a domineering Christian man who, I thought, was the answer to my prayers. How could I go wrong? Christians don't drink or smoke. Nor do they swear. Too late, I realized that I'd merely traded my parents' alcoholism for my husband's fanaticism. His narrow-mindedness fed his discontent, making it impossible to stay anywhere very long. The number of places in which we lived was exceeded only by the number of churches we attended. By the time I met Jim, I had become a spiritual, as well as a physical, vagabond.

Jim is an earthy man who swears, smokes, and drinks. But it is he who patiently distilled my childhood dreams and misplaced idealism into the essence of everyday reality. He brought order and stability into my life, no easy task. For, at the slightest sign of distress, his or mine, my impulse for years was to do as I'd always done—to run.

As if I were a wild bird suddenly trapped inside a building, I panicked and careened off the walls. My emotional wings flailed against what Jim had intended as my haven. Regardless of whether he understood me or not, he did not preach. He didn't nag or criticize. He simply went about his routine, showing by example the beauty of life lived on an even keel.

And he held me. He soothed my flightiness the way a trainer works a skittish animal. He gently anchored me until my own roots could take hold and sustain me. I no longer think about leaving, I've recently realized, because I no longer need that option. I am not going anywhere.

While Jim stabilized, Koochiching succored: wood to keep me warm in winter; food to feed my body year round; soil in which to sink my roots; peace to soothe my troubled spirit. Part of the reason it took me so long to feel at home here is that I had to overcome a lifetime of leavings.

The other reason was my disappointment in the Minnesota landscape. Like the child raised on television, I craved flashy western vistas where, within thirty minutes, one could drive from the dry lake bed of the Mojave Desert to the breathtaking hairpin curves on the back road of the San Bernardino Mountains. To me, the West's beauty was as accessible as those *National Geographic* photos; it wasn't even necessary to get out of the car to enjoy it.

Koochiching, however, does not go out of its way to impress anyone. Where we live there are no peaks or valleys, only the gentle rise and fall of a landscape scraped and nearly flattened by ancient glaciers. Koochiching's glacial heritage is that three-quarters of its now-wooded land is predominantly poorly drained lowlands: spruce swamps, floating bogs, and muskeg.

My first spring here, I was astounded by the sight of northern Minnesota waterways. In contrast to clear Western lakes and rivers, Koochiching's bog-filtered waters are as dark brown as my morning coffee. Where the Rapid River empties into Rainy River, the foam and water tumbling over the rocks look like boiling brown sugar. Bog tea, my neighbors call it.

For years my relationship with Koochiching was one of resignation. I lived here, but I didn't always like it. Our property is high and dry by northern Minnesota standards, yet its marginally useful heavy clay soil continues to challenge Jim's impressive gardening skills. It is land that defies my patience with the shovel and rake. Cheap, hundred-dollar-an-acre land that no one else wanted, land I've learned to love in spite of its stubbornness, in spite of myself. In the way it's taken years to get to know Jim—and to know myself—so it's taken me time to acquire an appreciation for the northern Minnesota landscape.

Koochiching. The word sounds as melodic and mysterious as the land for which it stands. Of difficult and uncertain meaning, it is from the Ojibwe language, interpreted as either "neighbor lake and river" or "a lake and river somewhere."

Now, at the top of the ladder, I push the heavy trapdoor open, grip the steel girders of the tower's point jutting into the center of the floor, and ease myself through the narrow opening. My backpack snags on the floor edge, but the tug does not set my heart to racing as it did when I first started working in the tower four years ago. My fearful reaction seems odd. Then, it felt as if some malicious spirit were yanking me from my perch. Today, I calmly work my shoulders back and forth, inching my loaded pack through the opening. One more rung, and I am in my cubicle.

From the DNR grounds below and twenty yards west of the base of my tower comes the sound of male voices. I open my southwest window and lean out, with my forearms on the ledge, into the crisp spring air to watch the four men of our fire crew. I take pleasure in watching the men go about their routine, I realize, because these people are as essential to my personal landscape as are the popple and spruce growing at the base of my tower. These are the friends and neighbors I never had before, even as Jim is my family.

Jim is tall and lanky, his curly, once-black hair now salted with white. His orientation toward the land was formed by the large, lean-spirited South Dakota farm family into which he was born, and by the exacting soil they worked. He is as methodical as the seasons, as purposeful, as resolute, as productive.

"Anybody who plants more than a dozen zucchini is crazy," I once told Jim in frustration as yet another armful of the shiny green produce appeared on my kitchen counter.

He looked genuinely shocked. "But," he said in his quiet voice, "I thought that was one of the most beautiful things I've done all year." I remember standing next to him, speechless (a rarity for me) and ashamed of my pettiness. Most of all I envied Jim's ability to see beauty in the ordinary. Therein, I knew, lay the peace for which I desperately yearned, a tranquility far beyond my reach.

As silly as it sounds, those were the times I felt like running away. Times I despaired of ever adjusting to an ordered way of life. I felt I'd been born with a missing synaptic link in my nervous makeup. I was programmed differently than Jim. My background had not prepared me for the tedium inherent in the sowing and reaping—and processing—according to the dictates of the seasons, rather than following those of mood or convenience.

Each year has gotten easier for me, but, like everything else about my Koochiching experience, my adjustment to the rigors of subsistence living has taken time. Time that I would not have allowed myself, if it hadn't been for Jim's steadying influence.

On his way to work now, our dispatcher pauses outside the office to talk with the four men. Mike Hanson is a striking figure because of his full, bushy red beard. He is the only one of us who was born and raised in Koochiching County. It pleases me to think that, because of our red hair and freckles, he and I could be mistaken for brother and sister. Family.

The screen door slams as he disappears into the office. Both Mike and I sign on at noon. It's time for work.

"Rapid River to Baudette, 10-8, visibility 20-plus." A familiar woman's voice breaks into my thoughts as the handheld radio placed on my narrow worktop crackles. As I am doing now, my counterpart stands in a tower identical to mine, twenty miles west of Birchdale and seven miles south of Baudette.

LaRae once intimidated me. Her mileages are accurate. She never gets confused, no matter how many smokes she's tracking during the course of the day. For years I have envied what I thought was LaRae's natural talent to know the land, an ability I despaired of acquiring.

What I didn't realize in those early days was that my handicap on my job had nothing to do with innate abilities, but with my unfamiliarity with the landscape. LaRae has worked the Rapid River tower for at least twenty years, I am told. Listening to her on the radio, it seems she knows the name of every road and every farmer within a fifteen-mile radius of her tower.

When I entered my tower, I was a stranger in every sense of the word. My alien status was emphasized every time I spoke over the radio as surely as if my speech were accented with Spanish or German. I sounded confused because I was. I knew few names of the people in our area, and had less of an idea where most of them lived. When Mike would radio that so-and-so had activated his burning permit—meaning I could soon expect to see smoke at that person's place—I often did not know where to begin looking.

Another difficulty is that, contrary to my expectations, my high vantage point does not provide an accurate visual image of the land. A mile and a half in either direction, Highway 11 disappears into the timber and the curvature of the earth. From that point on, the horizon flattens out. Distances compress so that a faint smoke five miles away looks deceptively similar to a larger smoke twenty miles distant.

After I stare at a particular spot for a few minutes, the tops of the timber blend together, reminding me of gently rolling desert sand dunes. From within that dense growth, I have few landmarks by which to judge distances. Surveying the landscape from my lofty perspective only confused my orientation of a land I was just beginning to learn from the ground.

Things began to make more sense to me this spring when I decided to write on the map. My handwriting now personalizes the plot-map abstraction of the landscape. I've scribbled people and place names at strategic points, along with the mileages between them. The bright yellow of a see-through marker highlights the section lines. The simple act of committing myself in writing has oriented me to the landscape, the way my well-adjusted binoculars aid my vision. Why I hesitated to mark on the map before this year baffles me. Perhaps it was instinctive, the mind-set of a woman who had never stayed in one place long enough to dare claim it as her own.

That I have somehow "connected" with my job, these people, and this place seems miraculous to me. In a way it is, because until recently, the long-ago loss of the sacred in my life cast a pall on every other aspect of my existence. Now, after years of spiritual free fall, I have finally acquired a way of relating to life, and to myself, that has nothing to do with adherence to creed or dogma. There is nothing rigid about what I believe, including a name by which to tag it. None is needed.

As the native Americans were comfortable with the ambiguity of the word *Koochiching*, "a lake and a river somewhere," I no longer require a rigid category or denomination with which to identify myself. My simple creed is my own: to walk as lightly on the earth, and to treat its creatures as gently, as is possible. All else seems to fall into place.

As I think of the spiritual in my life, my gaze comes to rest on the western horizon at 250 degrees. Two miles straight across the tops of the timber and across the willow-choked field south of our cabin is my backwoods sanctuary. It is a place of worship without walls, windows, pews, or collection plates. I can go there anytime, regardless of how I'm dressed. No one preaches. No one judges.

It is located several yards back into the woods and on a north-facing rock ridge. Not far from the rock is a white pine, a tree that was blown over many years ago and a large portion of its roots yanked from the soil. These roots, the size and shape of a chest-high, lacelike fan, now jut three feet into the air at a forty-five-degree angle from the ground. The main trunk now lies, quietly flourishing, stretched twenty feet across the forest floor.

From a distance, and before I noticed the root fan, I didn't realize it was anything other than a normal, healthy white pine. But the vertical portion, with its twelve- to fourteen-inch diameter trunk and long silky needles, is actually one of the tree's limbs. It sticks up into the air as straight, tall, and proud as the main trunk once stood.

Now the wind-direction indicator above my head squeaks as it shifts from northwest to southwest. The tower begins to vibrate in a low-key hum, the wind gently strumming the metal struts the way a musician strokes the strings of a guitar. A loose wire dings in accompaniment. In my early days in the tower, these sounds, especially during high winds, grated on my nerves. On those days I felt like running away.

But I stayed. And now the wind's song blends into the landscape that is my life here in Koochiching, as has the damaged white pine. That tree is special to me, because it matters not how far its seed traveled before it took root. Nor does it matter from where it came, whether its parent stood only one foot away, or miles. The important thing is that it did not perish during the windstorm that blew it over—and that it found the one spot of earth in which to anchor itself.

Like the pine, I am sustained by this place in northern Minnesota. Though it is not the landscape of my physical birth, Koochiching certainly is the birthplace of the woman I am today. I delight in the thought that there is something organic, almost primordial, in my having left the north bank of the Rio Grande only to settle on the south bank of the Rainy. I like to think that, in the way the juncos migrate on instinct, some inner prompting beyond my understanding led me to this large river. The circuitous route by which I arrived here is irrelevant. What matters is that I was fated to belong here—in the landscape that is Koochiching.

Open Spaces (excerpt)

Jim dale Huot-Vickery

My hand runs down the shaft of a canoe paddle in my cabin at Hocoka as my trails of power come to mind. It is late winter, after a long freeze-up, and my hopes are strong to visit once again North America's outback: its natural and wild areas, its national parks, lakeshores, wildlife refuges, and other open spaces.

Near my paddle are maps. There are maps of the Quetico-Superior canoe country in northeastern Minnesota and adjacent Ontario where I've lived eleven years. There are maps of Ontario's Wabakimi-Kopka country, the Albany River, and waterways further north. There are maps of New England's Thoreau country, the Pacific Northwest, and Alaska. Some are new. Others are worn and taped together. All are visual guides and food for dreams.

There is also, of course, one's internal mapless country—what John Muir biographer Michael Cohen calls the *pathless way*. Toward this I navigate. It cannot be helped. It is the way of mind and spirit leading to the most intriguing, most powerful landscape of all.

Still, I remain in love with real landscapes, open spaces, and the flow of wild rivers. I've hungered for and found the fluidity of life among wild shores in regions little known and relatively untrammeled.

Perhaps my fascination with landscapes and their effect on personal vision began when I was a boy. It was a subtle feeling coming with the turf and rivers of northwestern Minnesota. There at 48 degrees latitude, three hundred miles west of where I now sit, was the Red River Valley, the bottom of ancient glacial Lake Agassiz, larger in its prime than today's five Great Lakes combined. Boyhood pals and I roamed the valley's level plains. Although we knew dirt fields, we always ended up along rivers. There we found ourselves shuffling through cottonwood leaves along clay riverbanks, listening to brown water gurgle through weed-draped sweepers and watching thrown sticks—*splash*—float downstream.

They floated downstream to the Red River of the North, to Lake Winnipeg in Manitoba, then to the mighty Nelson River and Hudson Bay of the Arctic Ocean. Although we were at the center of the North American continent, we were connected to the sea.

As boys we bonded ourselves to the Clearwater River. We played cowboys and Indians on its banks, our knees scraping soil that had known white boys less than a hundred years. We'd get shot, each in our own turn, shot in the heart. I'd roll downhill toward the river, ending up limp but alive in the musty smell of crushed leaves and dry riverside grass.

We fished along the Clearwater, once seeing a snapping turtle large enough to bring tears of fear to a barefooted boy's eyes. We caught catfish ("Who'd ever eat 'em?" we chided each other), northern pike, bullheads, rock bass, and suckers. We brought some fish proudly home to the dinner table. Others we desecrated with jackknives as thoughtless boys do.

We sledded along the Clearwater, sliding down trails through woods on steep hills toward riverbanks. We skated on the Clearwater, sometimes racing cracking ice behind us or breaking through to a second layer of ice. Sometimes after heavy snows we would cross the river: skip the bridge, take the shortcut. We were leery of the slushy brown spots and the lively riffles of rapids that never knew ice. Although snow covered most of the Clearwater, it was always alive to us. ("People fall through," adults told us. "They get carried downstream under the ice by the current." Food for snapping turtles, we boys thought.) The river was always there: dark, sometimes frightening, yet always compelling with the wet spell of unseen events. Mystery.

Naturally it was in the Clearwater that I, at age nine, almost died.

I was standing in the river at a public swimming beach ("Don't you *dare* go swimming!" mother had said) and, upon turning, was astonished at how far I was from shore. Then I went under for no recallable reason. I just went under. Everything looked yellow, the color of urine or beer. I felt like I was floating in space . . . weightlessly spinning downstream under the Highway 32 bridge. I didn't need to breathe. It didn't matter.

Nor did it matter that I was drifting under the bridge toward rapids of a rock dam.

I was reborn on the beach.

A lifeguard had dragged me from the river. I was coughing. Choking. Soon crying. I stood up fuzzy-headed and turned toward a friend's riverside home where I was spending the weekend. I bumped into a tree and scraped sunburnt arms against roadside bushes. Then, there was a gravel road beneath my feet.

Good old gravel, I thought.

I revisited the Clearwater fifteen years later. Ken MacDonald and I were canoeing down the Red Lake River, having begun in my birthplace of Thief River Falls. We intended to paddle fifty miles in three days. As we passed Red Lake Falls we reached a shallow but swift bend where the Clearwater flowed lickety split into the Red Lake River on the left. I was reminded of how close I had come to death years earlier, of how life sometimes curls up like a frothing boil of whitewater in a constricted canyon.

From nature, by a heartbeat, comes flesh. From flesh and mind: awareness. From awareness: the sense, sometimes, of life as gift from mystery. But how is it, I asked myself (and still do), that rivers like the Clearwater flow through a person's life, like arteries, wearing grooves into the granite of boyhood-turned-manhood? Why does someone develop a thirst for *more* rivers? Why do people canoe, kayak, and raft down rivers like other people climb mountains? And how is it a person might grow up to seek a holy land, a special place to which and *through* which rivers flow?

Perhaps the answer is rooted in my appreciation of open space. I grew up relatively poor, and after forty years I see how being short on cash teaches something about public land and free-flowing rivers that is not learned otherwise.

I'm talking about the wealth of having places to roam and walk, to sit and dream, and to explore and harvest visions without trespassing. I'm talking about the sense of belonging, of being at home, of freedom and of self-realization. I'm talking, inevitably, about growth and happiness: the meat of fulfillment.

When my parents separated, my mother took custody of me and my three sisters. We never had enough money to buy land or a house, so we rented. We moved from one apartment house to another. There was scant feeling of home, of permanent shelter from rain and winter's subzero cold, a constant refuge, a place to draw the line and not be violated. *Our* place. No. If mom's rent check wasn't good we knew we could be out on the street.

This possibility of revocable tenancy bred in me a fondness for city, county, state, and federal public domains: the turf of "we the people." Open space. There I could explore riverbanks, cast my eye at the orange breasts of robins, listen to mourning doves sing above dawn dew, whittle sticks, and whistle a happy boy's songs.

Only in open space, I felt, was I free.

I thought of the public domain and the dynamics of trespassing one day, decades later, while I was canoeing in northern Minnesota's Voyageurs National Park. MacDonald and I, back in the canoe saddle together, faced large white-capped waves and were forced ashore near a private cabin. No one was home. We checked. We didn't intend to trespass. We just wanted to get off the water during gale-force winds.

Suddenly, as we sat on shore, a large motorboat roared across a narrows of Sand Point Lake. The driver stood up as he neared us.

"Get the hell out of here!" he yelled, no questions asked. "Get out!"

Although he was guarding a friend's property, playing police-man, his words struck home. We were reluctant to leave but got back in our canoe and pushed off into dangerous waters.

Eviction.

Private versus public.

Later I was on a four-mile walk near Blackduck in north central Minnesota. It had been a long drive from Ely, Minnesota, through a tunnel of fog and bog to visit my mother over Christmas. I needed to stretch my legs. When I reached the local golf course I headed across open terrain. I stopped at a green and scraped its snow-dusted surface with the toe of my boot.

"Get off the green!" a man yelled from the driveway of a nearby house. He had gotten out of an El Camino with a realty name em-blazoned on its doors. "Go away! Get off the green!"

I headed across the golf course. I seethed. Again I was a tres-passer. Again I felt the noose tighten around my need to roam.

Unable then to own land or a home, I wanted—at least—a place to walk, camp, watch wildlife, to be at peace and not feel alien in my own country. This was my, and every American's, alleged birth-right. In time I judged my standard of living not by what I had but by the quality and size of open space around me.

When we whites, after all, swept across the North American continent we took possession of the land. We fenced it off as though barbed wire came with the Bible. We devised property lines, made and mounted No Trespassing signs, and herded the continent's natives, the resistance, onto boundaried reservations. Altogether we laid an abstract Anglo-Saxon grid of land owner-ship over the water, forest, and wind-rippled grass. For those who couldn't adjust to that grid: tough. When it came to land, if you didn't own it, if you hadn't put your John Hancock on the right papers, you didn't belong on it.

Damn the free spirit.

"*Get the hell out of here*," the man had said.

Against this backdrop it was difficult for me to empathize with people screaming about federal land grabs involving national parks, wildlife refuges, and wilderness areas. Those who complained most about government protection or expansion of the federal domain were usually landowners who had a piece of the rock. Or they were people who might benefit financially by selling to individuals, thus commercially exploiting what could belong to everyone. It was my freedom from No Trespassing signs that some of the landed gentry threatened. It was the need of people like myself to saunter unmolested that they couldn't, or wouldn't, comprehend.

So how could I oppose public ownership of land?

As long as people were not locked out of open spaces, those spaces were gifts to the spirit. Not luxuries, but necessities. Not mere superfluous playgrounds, but commonly held homes for the needy freedoms of man.

I am not a man who gladly stands with his face or back to walls. This I understood as I gravitated over the years to the open spaces of North America. I wanted to know their freedoms and the texture of their landscape and watershed. There were the Basswood River, Maligne, Little Missouri, Little Fork, Kaministikwia, Big Fork, Kawishiwi, Kopka, Greyson, Horse, Dog, and other rivers. They formed for me, and still do, a metaphorical web of rivers flowing to and from a common center like liquid spokes of a wheel undulating in space: the space of my dreams, the hub of my hopes. The rivers radiate light, and the light bathes my eyes in silver water.

I call it my river mandala.

This mandala is not merely a literary doily. It is as real for me as a guiding vision, and it's just as powerful. It evokes change and growth. I scan the stars for it on clear nights. I sniff it out among pistils of pollinating wildflowers on hot midsummer noons. At dusk, when I close my eyes in the cabin loft, my feet toward the east as Sioux once lay, I sense the mandala's vibrant presence. It is around me and in me.

I'm at peace with it, and in the best of times it leads me to joy.

As fanciful as my river mandala appears, however, it is rooted in real landscapes with innate power. Landscapes affect people. They enlarge vision. They build strength. They expand the limits of geographical awareness. When as adventurers we pass through landscapes, we move through color, sound, smells, light, shade, taste, and vegetative texture; our bodies swim through a cacophony of sensations. There is sometimes risk and danger as flesh dances with ecosystems and climate. There are encounters with people who live so close to landscapes that they seem one with them, and, truly, they are. The fortunate adventurer returns home a different person, subtly better, forever branded, having been worked upon. Impressed. Whether we are alert adventurers or people who awaken to and dwell in one landscape, we enter a chrysalis and emerge, like Thoreau from Walden Pond, more perfect creatures.

Do we not become in part manifestations of where we've been and lived our days? Do we not respond physically and psychologically, if not spiritually, to our environments? Will not March's hoar-frosted trees I see out my cabin window, or the snow-covered lake's brilliant whiteness, affect my outlook tonight and tomorrow? Does a person ever lose the trees, animals, skies, and sunrises of his or her outdoor hours? Or do these things forever provide us with a living mosaic of natural beauty that nourishes awe, if not hope, during mankind's sometimes grim search for meaning?

I think they do.

This, then, is my bias: We can nurture contact with nature in the hope of attuning ourselves to an ever-evolving wholeness and discovery, or we can risk death by alienation.

Collectively, the choice is ours.

Listening for the Esker's Song

Anne Marie Erickson

It was late autumn. It was dusk. I was the only person there. A friend had told me about Scenic State Park near Bigfork. "There's a beautiful trail between two lakes," she said. On my park map, a small star marked a narrow peninsula called Chase Point, which snaked between Coon and Sandwick Lakes. The legend told me that this is "a unique natural feature."

A steep hill crested by tall red and white pines marked the entrance to the peninsula. The path, worn like the steps to an old cathedral, sank between gentle slopes.

Broad boughs canopied the pathway as I descended into a dark cedar grove. Ahead, the ridge swung sharply to the west and narrowed. Its steep flanks bristled with cedar, pine, and paper birch. A branch cracked; I spotted a deer grazing down by the shore.

I picked my way around bare roots and whalebacked rocks. A pair of gray jays glided between the trees ahead, as if they were my guides. Two close-growing pines marked a passageway. I stepped between them.

The flat-backed ridge curved north and narrowed once again.

Slim red pines surged up the steep embankment and filled the trail. The ground glowed with the rust of fallen pine needles. The low sun striped their ruddy bark pale gray and gold. In the vague light, the smallest trees looked like reeds swaying underwater.

It was a mile-long walk out to the peninsula's brow, which stood sixty feet above the lakes. A flight of stairs led down to the shore. I walked with care; the weathered steps seemed to drift in the dusk. Cedar trees bowed toward the dark water. The high ridge loomed behind me.

It *was* a beautiful trail. But it was something more. It was a place where the earth sloped sharply upward. When I walked the esker's hunched back, I had been treading on a spine of the earth.

This winding ridge is one of the more remarkable scars that glaciers left on the land ten thousand years ago. Chase Point "is believed to be an old esker," according to a park brochure. Eskers were shaped by sands deposited in the beds of subglacial streams. The streams carried meltwater from a downwasting glacier. Where I had walked a stream had once tunneled, ice pressing in on its sides.

Esker—a curious word, I think—comes from the Old Irish *escir.* Another name, *os,* is from an Old Norse word for *ridge.* Eskers occur in Ireland, Scotland, Scandinavia, and Canada, and in the northern United States.

Most eskers are found in areas of low relief. They stand high above the surrounding lowlands like earthen forts; perhaps that is why they seem unnatural.

In a data-filled guide to Minnesota geology, fanciful words like *fairyland, mysterious,* and *enchanting* are used to describe Chase Point. The word *enchant* comes from the Latin *cantare* (to sing). And *mystery* is a truth knowable only through divine revelation.

In telephone conversations with geologists around the state, I was struck by the gentle voices of the men. I wanted to learn more about eskers. The geologists helped me visualize Chase Point when it was a tunnel beneath a mile of ice. I felt the claustrophobic's panic. Inside the esker, they say, you will find clean, water-sorted sands. The image is so orderly. It eases the panic.

Perhaps humility tempers the geologists' voices. They know that if geologic time were measured like the annual rings of an ancient tree, we would locate ourselves in the thin outermost ring. Behind us, the aeons spin inward.

The most eloquent voice is that of the man who manages the park. He tells me that the only Native American artifacts found in the immediate area were on Chase Point. "It's a culturally significant site," he says. Then he pictures a campsite, high on the ridge, lake breezes cooling the summer travelers. "There are a lot of cedars and shrubs on Chase Point that the deer chew on. I've seen the wolves chase deer down the steep banks of the esker in the winter, and corner them there. Perhaps the Ojibwe used the same hunting technique.

"White settlers may well have stopped and camped overnight at this place, too," he says. "There is very little high ground in this area other than the parklands. It would have been a natural route for pioneers as they traveled to Bigfork from the southeast." They came to settle one of the last great pine frontiers.

In 1921 Bigfork's citizens asked state officials to establish what is now Scenic State Park. They wanted to preserve the virgin stands of red and white pine. "This park is here because of the vision of the people," the park manager tells me. "Man has been appreciating beauty since time began."

Walt Whitman said that "poets don't have to tell folks what beauty is, folks know well enough what beauty is. The poet must indicate the path between reality and men's souls." Folks knew that the pine-topped esker, shouldering its way between two lakes, was worth preserving. People gravitate toward certain places, as if the land calls to them.

I'm drawn to powerful landscapes. The rocky west coasts of Norway and Ireland. The dry mountains of Spain. Northern Minnesota's boreal forests. These are not easy places in which to live. Inishmore's farmers haul seaweed to build soil on the Irish limestone. My Norwegian cousins terrace small hay fields into the mountain behind the family homeplace. Regiments of olive trees march up Andalusia's arid red slopes.

Here, we have deep winters and dense woods. The few farmers tend small fields, ever watchful for encroaching aspen.

Each landscape has its song, waiting to be sung. Andalusia's traditional "deep song" (*cante hondo*) is somber, fierce, and lonely. It's both a proud Spanish paean and a lament. Hardanger fiddles sing old Norwegian tunes. Beneath the gay melody, a second set of strings drones a doleful, eerie song. A wild longing whirls inside an Irish reel.

The song of this esker is Ojibwe. A chorus of strong male voices cries above a throbbing drum. It is the pulse I feel beneath the esker's spine. The men sing their story with a high wail, like old women keening at a wake. Much of the song is pure sound; the words have been forgotten.

Once I passed through an urban shopping mall during "ethnic diversity" week. A group of Ojibwe men, dressed in blue jeans and plaid shirts, sat on metal folding chairs in the mall's center. They circled a bass drum laid on its side. One young girl waited to dance.

The men struck the drum. The lead singer exhaled a descending spiral of sound; the others finished his phrase in a raw unison. The girl glided along the circle's edge. She twirled. Her bright shawl feathered the air.

The drumming and singing grew more forceful. It rang against shop walls. It pummeled the exotic flowers, French silk hosiery, and imported leather shoes. I thought their song would cause the walls to crumble. Surely, everything must stop—the escalators frozen in their silvery ascent, the cash registers suddenly locked shut.

The song of the esker is Ojibwe. It is a summons to memory. It vibrates with the passion of loss.

Geologists say that they "believe" Chase Point is an esker. They have never done the necessary soil sampling to declare with certainty that it is one. I believe that a ridge near our home is an esker.

Twenty years ago our neighbors had looked down from that ridge and were delighted. They bought the farm. "We share the same ridge," said an early visitor to their place, by way of introduction.

They learned their land's secret places—the little shrubs of Labrador tea hunched in a bog, the chanterelle's orange flare brightening a grove. The esker was the place to enter into mysteries. When friends gathered to celebrate the autumnal equinox, we were led to the high wooded ridge behind their barn.

We ascended by lantern light, guided by our sure-footed hosts. A bonfire welcomed us. The group circled the fire and paused at each cardinal point. East, south, west, then north, the source of our powerful winters. We faced the long, hummocky back of the esker. Above it, clear white light from long-dead stars winked down on us.

Our neighbors are gone now, divorced, and the place sits empty. In autumn, my husband and I clear fallen trees in preparation for skiing. The trail ends at the farm's ridge. At its highest point, the narrow esker stands a sheer forty feet above our hay field. The western slope, crowded with balsam, birch, and aspen, is more gradual. It overlooks a tangle of swampland.

A local dealer in sand and gravel has offered to buy the farm. He tells me that he scouts for gravel pits by reading the lay of the land: "I look for ridges or banks." He doesn't know what an esker is.

The farm's esker runs to the southeast, angling toward the Mississippi River. South of the farm, large shovels already eat away the esker's midsection.

An abandoned gravel pit lies northwest of the esker. It was depleted years ago. I wonder what the land looked like before the gravel was mined. Now it's a broad, flat basin—a good place to pick wild raspberries or to do some target practice. A large piece of iron has settled into the brush. Cardboard boxes sag nearby. Boulders are pushed to one side; we used to come here in the blue pickup and load some of them up. They are cemented into our home's stonework foundation.

A geologist tells me that there are a lot of eskers in this part of the state, but most of them are not accessible. Many have never been mapped. "There's plenty of other gravel around. But you have to dig to find it," he says. "I'd sure hate to see a wonderful thing like an esker hauled away in dump trucks."

His words recall the awe I felt when I first walked Chase Point. I stood on the esker's shore, bowed low like one of the cedar trees, its flat leaves brushing the lake. I clung to the edge; the esker loomed above me. Dark waters waited below.

The esker had led me on a path between reality and my soul. I heard its ancient song and felt dread, the dark twin of awe.

I had not come as a pilgrim. There were no drums to beat away the silence. I came modern, walking to the esker from my car. I left humbled by the spirit of the place.

The Tourist

Pauline Brunette Danforth

One day you come across childhood photographs of yourself wearing plastic Indian gear and fluorescent feathers. You are about ten years old in the picture, almost past the age of make-believe, but also too young to question the appropriateness of your getup. Your slight scowl hints at your reluctance in posing.

Being a thoughtful man now, you contrast this to the Indians you pass sitting in doorways along Franklin Avenue. You drive this Minneapolis street daily on your way to work. Now that winter is over, you've noticed many of them walking in small groups, turning their sometimes ravaged faces away from the graffitied buildings and toward the warm spring sun. Perhaps you wonder how they came to be here, so far from what you perceive as their noble heritage.

Besides being thoughtful, you are curious. You take out the map and decide to visit an Indian reservation, just to see for yourself how "real Indians" live. You send away for a few of those "Explore Minnesota" tourism brochures and are immediately drawn to the Indian chief nobly looking over the Mississippi headwaters at Itasca

State Park. The flyer says the park has an "Indian village," so you decide to go there first, then drive through the nearby White Earth Reservation.

Not long after, on another of those promising spring days, you start off. You drive north up Highway 10, then at the town of Wadena you turn onto 71. You wonder at the town's name, never imagining it refers to a prominent Chippewa leader from Mille Lacs who traveled through the region en route to the White Earth Reservation, which was intended to be the final home of all the Chippewa in Minnesota. (Chippewa is one of several names given to the Indians living on seven northern Minnesota reservations. Other names include Ojibwe and Anishinaabe, their tribal name.)

You probably don't know that much of Minnesota, including Itasca State Park, was claimed by the Chippewa, and was as much their home as the White Earth Reservation land set aside by the 1867 treaty. After all, your fifth grade history class taught you very little about Indians, or the Chippewa in particular, except that their history began with their being conquered. So you drive northward on roads that follow ancient trails, not comprehending all the people who traveled this way before.

You enter Itasca State Park through the eastern gate and marvel at its wonderful name. Itasca sounds rough and brave, and probably is named after some chieftain, you comment aloud. Pulling over at the ranger station, you ask and are surprised to learn it comes from *veritas caput,* Latin for "true head," in reference to its being the headwaters of the great Mississippi River.

As you drive through the park you recall that the park area was "discovered" by Henry Rowe Schoolcraft, but how are you to know that he was brought here by an Ojibwe Indian named O-zha-wun-dib and that for a century Ojibwe and Dakotas hunted here and gathered wild rice and berries, and even before that Cheyenne and Arapaho lived here?

You drive the narrow road into the park and momentarily forget your mission to meet real Indians. High above you, shading the mature forest, are tall, majestic pines. You open your window and trail your hand in the breeze. Across from Preacher's Grove, you pull over onto the narrow shoulder. Impulsively, you get out of your car and climb down a little hill. Suddenly you find yourself surrounded by cedar trees, enveloped by the warmest, sweetest smell you've ever experienced. You stand and close your eyes and inhale slowly and smile contentedly.

Continuing your journey, you arrive at the park headquarters. You see an exhibit explaining Indian-white relations in the fur trade, but instead of looking, you scan the postcard rack and choose one with an Indian wrapped in a blanket. You don't notice the photo has a desert background, quite unlike the tall trees that surround you now.

Yes, instead of reading those little placards, you decide you want to see the real thing. The ranger said there is an Indian now at the Mississippi headwaters, in full costume, and for five dollars you can get your photograph taken with him so your grandchildren will see that you truly did meet real Indians in northern Minnesota.

You walk a little way through the pines. There he is now, a medium-height, overweight man, slightly balding and speaking perfectly good English. He doesn't look much like you imagined; after all, aren't the "real" Indians tall and lean with long black braids? How are you to know that Schoolcraft and his friends left more than footprints when they visited tribal people? They contributed to the gene pool, and that explains the balding. You don't know that the man's weight is probably due to years of commodities— government surplus foods high in fat and cholesterol, canned beef meat swimming in salt and fat, white lard used to fry government-issue flour into fry bread. That's really why this disappointing Indian is fat.

The Indian puts on his long, flowing headdress. This pleases you. In full regalia, he looks every bit the chief. He even calls himself Chief Big Wind. If you asked him, he might confide that he commissioned his headdress. It didn't come down from his grandfather as you want to believe. He might tell you headdresses were worn by plains Indians and if you looked at old government photos, you'd notice that the Indians were wearing turkey feathers, probably at the insistence of a photographer who believed all Indians belonged in feathers.

He probably won't tell you this, nor will he tell you that his friends make fun of his name. He made it up. His friends laugh and speculate about what else he's telling the tourists, like maybe that his great-great-grandfather swam out to meet the Mayflower. Yes, depending on the honesty of your chief, you might leave disappointed, but most likely he will leave you in the dark; after all, you are only a tourist who wants to meet a real made-in-Hollywood Indian.

Leaving Itasca State Park, you take Highway 113. The hills and curves sway you and your car in rhythmic motion past sun-dappled lakes and shaded groves. The locals would tell you it has 113 curves between where it branches off Highway 71 and where you turn south on it to the town of White Earth. You might even count them yourself, but instead you admire the sparkling lakes: Bad Medicine, Long Lost Lake, and others too small to be real Minnesota lakes.

You slow down. You enjoy the drive. After all, you don't know the real reasons why the road has so many curves. The history of this road, the knowledge that its path was chosen by the lumbermen claiming Indian lands isn't written in history books. You have no way of knowing that the best timber was identified and the road built through the Indian homesteads to get at that timber. Naively, you do wonder aloud why the Indians didn't conserve some big trees, like the majestic white pines you just saw in the park.

Gradually, you notice fewer pine trees and more open, rolling hills. Cresting on the horizon, you pull over onto the graveled shoulder. You get out and survey the vast unending farm fields. You feel the heat of the midday sun and admire how it makes the young alfalfa shimmer as it gently bends in the slight breeze. You imagine the undulating fields stretching as far as the Red River Valley, and maybe beyond.

Well, you've come to the turnoff to White Earth, governing center to this reservation, once thirty-six townships in size, now reduced by illegal land transactions at the turn of the century to less than one-tenth of that size. Those neat farms you see and all those resorts whose signs beckon you off course aren't owned by Indians. Innocently, you expect reservations are where Indian people live, not all the descendants of the immigrants who bought a piece of it from land speculators, who in turn bought it for a song and a dime from the Indian allottees.

The Indian housing is coming up soon. That cluster of houses there, an unnatural quasi-urban community, was built because it was easier and cheaper for the government to build twenty identical homes in one tight spot than to build homes on scattered sites that respected people's original homesteads. You see how old those houses look, and they were only built ten years ago. Shoddy workmanship and materials. If you struck up a conversation with one of the old men sunning themselves out front, they might complain about the "deal" cut by the tribal council. Most likely, though, if you stopped they would figure you were lost and would direct you to the main highway out of town.

Continuing on your way, you take a left past some government-looking buildings. A small sign tells you it's the Public Health Clinic. The parking lot is full of old cars and beat-up pickups, some with doors that don't match, most of them sporting bumper stickers proclaiming "Ojibwe and Proud" and "Fry Bread Power."

On a whim, you decide to stop. Maybe you are a doctor and that car ride gave you indigestion. You figure the hospital would have a pharmacy. Besides, you still want to meet "real Indians" and you figure there would be some in the clinic. You don't know that the really sick Indians hesitate to use Public Health because lots of people have stories about relatives whose symptoms were ignorantly blamed on poor hygiene—or worse, they had an aunt who saw one of the doctors here for several months before they referred her to a specialist in Fargo who diagnosed advanced cancer. You don't know that most of the doctors here know as little as you do about the lives of the local Indian residents.

You enter and ask a dark-haired nurse's aide if they have a pharmacy where you can purchase an antacid. She says they give Indians free care, but can only treat white people if it's an emergency. You agree you're in no grave danger of dying, but decide to sit a minute.

You note that the doctors are all white and in a hurry. You want to know more about the hospital, but if that happened you would again be disappointed. If one of the young doctors took time to talk to you, he would tell you he owes two years to this godforsaken place for school loans, then he is off to his father's practice in Minnetonka. He would tell you that he is overworked and underpaid and is counting the days until he can leave.

If he did talk to you and was in a good mood, he might tell you about the old woman who comes in for her diabetes and tells him about the herbs that help her arthritis. But the doctor doesn't have time for a friendly chat, so you don't know all these things about his life. You only see lots of tired brown faces and busy, distracted white ones.

In the hubbub of patients—young mothers comforting sick, crying children, and dirty-jeaned middle-aged men who can't see their belt buckles—one elderly woman stands out. She is sitting there patiently, her eyes following a young child silently putting together a puzzle on the floor before her. You see her round face reflected in the shape of the child's, and you know that is her grandchild. You wonder where she's been in life and what secrets she holds.

You rest a minute, thinking these are "real Indians," unlike the chief at Itasca State Park. You leave the hospital and comment on your way out to the nurse, "It's so nice for the Indians to have a free clinic."

Once in your car, you study the map and outline your trip following the western edge of the reservation north to Mahnomen through Ogema and Waubun. The names are melodious and you wonder what they mean, but unless you ask someone, you'll never know that Ogema means leader, Waubun means sunrise, and Mahnomen refers to that native rice that grows so abundantly around here. Driving along the two-lane highway, you pass a lot of semis and notice the tall round silos that dot the landscape.

The nearly flat land, vast and open, is beautiful but much different from the rolling hills and tall pine trees you admired earlier. Already you love this land of contrasts and wonder how the Indians living here could move to the concrete canyons of the Cities.

Mahnomen is your destination. You want to visit Shooting Star, the new casino. You see it as you enter town from the south. Its dazzling neon lights beckon you with promises of "Indian crafts" and the "best buffet this side of Fargo." Tour buses with North Dakota, South Dakota, and even Manitoba license plates form a barrier by the front entrance. Shiny cars bearing White Earth Reservation license plates form a second line in an area marked "Reserved."

When you enter, your eyes adjust to the fluorescent and neon lights, which dim in comparison to the sunshine outside. Middle-aged men and women, many of them Indian, lean on the stools next to the quarter machines. Courteous staff with tags bearing the names Bellanger, Beaulieu, Fairbanks, and Littlewolf remind you of the mixed French, English, and Chippewa ancestry of this reservation. They offer you coffee, soft drinks, and quarter change. Other staff members drift by picking up trash almost before it lands on the plush carpeted floor.

You think of the money flowing through this place and think of those fancy cars parked out front. You don't know that the average wage paid here is barely above minimum wage and many drive up to sixty miles each way to work here. You don't know that the big Buicks and fancy vans in the parking lot belong to an elite group of tribal leaders, not to the people picking up trash and giving out change. No, if you eavesdropped on those men over there stand-ing in a tight knot of faded jean jackets, you would hear about the federal investigation into the management of this casino.

Well, you don't know what they are saying, so you leave believ-ing this fancy casino is making life easier on this reservation.

You drive through the dusty farm town of Mahnomen, deserted now at five in the afternoon. You pass a John Deere farm imple-ment dealer, a feed and grain store, a couple of churches, and the Red Apple Cafe. Down a flat, tree-shaded street you find the bed and breakfast you are staying at. With wide-eyed appreciation, you admire the solid wood exterior. You didn't expect a house up here to be so grand.

Your host lets you in, leading you through oak doorways, past shiny maple furnishings. He tells you that J. W. Teague built this house during the height of the lumbering days. You admit knowing about James Hill's lumbering legacy in Minnesota but don't recog-nize the Teague name. Your host explains that a lot of small-town lumbermen supplied the building trade in Minneapolis and St. Paul, and he wouldn't be surprised if this same timber built some of the fine old homes that grace the Summit Hill neighborhood.

You settle into your room with its gingham café curtains and look around. The bed is covered by a white tufted bedspread. The springs squeak loudly as you bounce on the edge. On the heavy oak bureau you see a framed photograph of Theodore Roosevelt shaking hands with a feathered Indian. You step closer to look and then notice a small closet in the far corner of the room.

The door is rather low. You open it, scrunch down, and sit in the middle of the empty closet. It smells deliciously like the woods you walked in earlier today. You close your eyes and imagine that old woman you studied at the clinic today. You imagine her in those woods, and even though the doctor didn't tell you this, you imagine her walking through that cedar swamp you smelled earlier. You see her walking in her faded calico dress, her senses bent toward the earth, looking for just the right herbal medicine.

Gray-haired and arthritic, she bends down, hand clutching her government-issue cane, and delicately plucks that flowering herb that will make her grandchild sing again. She is happy. You have no way of knowing this, but you see, even though you are just a tourist, the fact that you've left your comfortable city home to visit this place shows you are curious and you have an imagination and a heart to see people who are different.

Burial

Kent Nerburn

My home is over there.
Now I remember it.
TEWA SONG

I am standing before a northern lake on a windswept point of land as a young Indian boy I know is lowered into the earth by his friends and family. It is a strange and lonely funeral—they all are, in their own way. But this boy was a friend of mine, and the loss has struck me with unusual force.

He was a quiet sort who kept his counsel except to joke occasionally when he was joshed or teased. He had been a boxer, a good one, but had given it up and had taken, as his grandmother told me, to staying up all night and lifting weights at three in the morning. He drank, would not talk to her, became sullen and distant. So great was his mask that soon all chose to ignore him. But, as with all hidden faces, his shone with a special grace when in those unguarded moments it opened with a warm and honest smile. These smiles are what I remember about him.

The funeral was typical of his native community. Babies cried.

People smoked cigarettes. The coffin stood in the center of a dingy community gym while people sat around the outside edges on bleachers, like spectators at a basketball game. The family and friends—honored guests and deepest mourners—were on folding chairs facing the casket. One part of the gym was given over to a potluck, and each person stopped briefly and scraped a bit of food into a box to be placed before the grave so the departing spirit would have nourishment on its journey to the afterlife. The head man of the community, who was also the spiritual leader, spoke only briefly in English before turning to Ojibwe.

Young girls cried. Young men stared at the ceiling. As the words were finished, the door to the outside was pushed open and the casket was wheeled forward into the shaft of intruding daylight. The head man shook a rattle and chanted a low mournful prayer that sounded almost like a lullaby. A circle of men began drumming and singing. Amid much grunting and shouted direction, the casket was wrestled out through the door and onto the bed of a waiting pickup truck to be carried to the lonely promontory where the boy would be laid to rest among his ancestors.

The wind was warm. The sky was an empty blue. Leaves had fallen, but the memory of summer warmth was everywhere. It was a good day to die.

I have lived, now, for years in this northwestern part of Minnesota, this forgotten corner of our country, where the prairies meet the woodlands, the Mississippi starts its course, and the water changes flow from south to north. This is not a gentle place, but neither is it heroic. It is ruminative, reflective, a land of changes, where one cannot believe too strongly in the joys of summer or the trials of winter, because the turning of the seasons is ever present in the mind.

It is a land of harsh realities. Settlers who stopped in this place were unable to find an easy rest. They chose it because they were the outlaws, the misfits, the desperately poor, or those who had to rage and measure themselves against some brutal but indifferent god. Men became suspicious; women became depressed. The earth gave but little, and what it gave came grudgingly. Rocks pushed like cruel jokes through the impoverished soil and mocked the efforts of the farmers to bring forth crops from the sun-starved ground.

This was not my native home. I was born farther to the south, though not by much. But my childhood was under spreading trees, not in the darkness of the pines. To come to this land was to discover something new, more brooding, deeper, almost sinister. It was a life of contrasts: dark forests, bright lakes; harsh winters, indolent summers. People huddled close to the earth and lived their lives in frenzied spasms of activity when for a few short months the sunfall days blew dappled through the summer pines.

Death was a way of life here, from gunshot, from freezing, from wandering off in the middle of winter, from despair. People killed to live, and they lived to kill. Hunting was religion; fishing, worshipful sport. In the fall, deer carcasses hung from tripods made of logs. Stringers of fish were displayed proudly, and young boys were told that in their skill at killing lay their manhood.

It repelled me, and it fascinated me. There was an elemental grandeur somewhere in this way of living, but it was submerged under brutishness and too often celebrated for its squalid resistance to anything ennobling or full of grace. Greatness had no shape beyond the number of trees that could be sheared from the land or the profusion of pelts that could be hung from a pole. Courage was embodied in the logger who dragged himself five miles through the forest and the snow after accidentally severing his leg with a chain saw.

Civilization was under siege or, at best, present in its most rudimentary form. Often I have wanted to escape.

But civilization is a malleable concept. Other voices speak as well. This is also Indian land. Its marshy surfaces and low-lying, scrubby cover made it rich in bounty for those who hunted and gathered as a way of life. And its stolid resistance to tilling has kept the full force of white settlement away. Even now the reservations surround the towns and serve as ghostly reminders that we who have come from other shores are still but visitors here, understanding only dimly the ways of the land that we have appeared to conquer.

In the Indians who have made their home here—like my young departed friend—something lives that invests this harsh land with spiritual value. It is not some romantic taproot into primeval forest mysteries and pre-Adamic unities with nature. It is far more integrated, far more resolved and inseparable from their character. Their furtiveness fits perfectly with the dark corners of the forest. Their judgmental ways are in keeping with the demanding indifference of the land. Their silence suits the distances; their way of thinking meanders like the trails on the hillsides and the oxbows in the creeks. In their fatalism one senses the turning of the seasons, a peaceful acquiescence devoid of pessimism and despair.

It is akin to a Taoist understanding, but with a darker musk, where nature is not merely the reflection of a life well lived, but is the very crucible from which all understanding comes. Animals are teachers, the landscape shapes personal psychology, and the dominant natural forces are the point of contact with deity and the template of spiritual understanding.

Far from seeming brutish, the native people seemed grounded and resolved, and their lack of civilization felt more like an integration into nature than a failure to conquer its rough forms.

Several years ago, the boy laid out before me was part of a group that I brought to visit the man who now stands over him giving the final benediction. It was an organized attempt to bring the voice of the elders to the ears of the youth. The elder spoke of the traditional ways of teaching: how an infant was carried on the back, facing out, so it might see where the mother has been and thus gain knowledge of the mother's daily life; how the hands were swaddled, so the child must learn stillness and how to observe;

how the infant was placed upright, beneath a tree, so it would have as its constant companion the movements of the wind.

He told them of the animals, of how the bear was observed in order to see which plants were safe to eat, how the wolf was taken as the model of fidelity, and how the eagle was studied for its ways of raising the young.

The young people fidgeted and stared. They whispered to each other. The old man was going on too long.

Like an animal going back into the forest, he closed his eyes, turned inward, and was gone.

We have on this land a clash of genius. The European, logical heir to the Greeks, the Romans, the Christian in all its forms, brought to these shores a faith in progress, a teleology of hope. It is a fine and noble instinct, too quickly denigrated these days, that finds truth in movement, in discovery, in examination, in a promise of perfectibility. It is the motive force of evolution, the engine of exploration, the philosophical extrapolation of the way we experience time.

Yet there are other ways. The cyclical, the circular, the great gyre of repetitive ritual is also written in the earth in which we live. The planets, wheeling through time, the seasons, repeating their eternal liturgy, speak of a past that is always alive in the present, and an earth revealed by ever more acute understanding of analogy.

The mandala and the medicine wheel, as surely as the quest for the grail, reveal a path of spiritual understanding.

My young friend was caught in between. His progress had been too slow, his faith in the eternal lessons of nature too weak a balm. He had lived his life suspended between truths, and in the end neither had been strong enough to save him.

He is being buried in his traditional garb. His face is painted; he is wearing feathers. Loving, grieving hands have laid him out, dressed him, and prepared him in the traditional way, far from antiseptic funeral parlors and stainless steel gurneys and bottles of fluids. He is being sent off with rattles and chants that he only dimly understood, to an afterlife in which he only half-believed.

These are not easy days. We stumble on the foundations of our faith. Our belief in the rational demands first principles, from which all must logically evolve. Yet our need for life is so strong, our faith in Being so immutable, that we want creators, intercessors, presences in our lives.

We want our belief inhabited by logic, but we also want it infused with life and personal contact, and, lacking both, we cry out like the desperate man in the Gospels, "I believe, I believe. Help my unbelief."

They are placing him in the earth now. The hole is not squared. It was dug by friendly hands, not by those who make a business of interment. They lower the casket on rope slings; if they let one slip, he will spill out. People sit on hoods of cars, smoking cigarettes, waiting. The birds fly overhead. So large a gathering makes them curious. Perhaps they sense the presence of death.

Beneath our days, beneath our community, beneath even our culture and our history, lies a layer of meaning. It has a logic, and it has a life. It pivots on the movements of the stars and pulsates with the drumbeat of the seasons. Here thunder shapes the voice of God; the birds reveal the ways of motherhood. Plants scream when they're pulled and flourish when they're exposed to song. Our strength reflects what the landscape demands; rocks reveal the shape of protection. The spirits of our fathers put a face upon our courage, and bears teach men to dance. Life is lived in a symphony of revelation, and children learn to fear the shadow or to celebrate the light.

The boy is in the earth now. We walk up, one by one, and shovel a mound of dirt into the hole. It echoes hard and hollow on the casket. The young men—his friends—jump in the hole and pack soil around the sides. They are forceful, abrupt, alive with the importance of their task.

The old man steps to the side of the grave. He lights the pipe, offers smoke in the four directions, toward mother earth, toward father sky. He speaks, low, in Ojibwe. I recognize the word for bear, the word for eagle. The others' heads are bowed, as they are at all places, in all times, in the presence of death.

The old man places the tobacco, the sacred herb, in the grave. It comes from the earth, it rises to the heavens. It follows all laws of those who would return to God.

We cannot find our lives in weights and measures.

Microscopes and telescopes increase our context; they do not find origins or conclusions. Like the spirit we brought to this land, they probe, they examine, they explore. "Meaning," they proclaim, "is beyond our vision. Truth is below our sight."

But there is research of a different sort. It does not move, it does not seek. It watches until stillness shifts or silence makes a sound. It drinks in a universe whose origin and every manifestation is alive, and whose every movement demonstrates its laws. What exists beyond our boundaries is not unknown; it simply is not revealed.

A final prayer is offered. The young men shape the earth into a mound above the grave—the geometry of folded hands, of pyramids, of pines.

I turn and walk away. For me, it is finished. To stay longer would be false and intrusive, an arrogance uncalled for by the moment. What remains is hidden, closed to me by the barriers of culture. My presence here has been enough.

I walk toward the waning sun. I turn once toward the east, toward the secrecy of the forests, once toward the west, where the prairies come alive with autumn light. I turn south to where the

Mississippi starts the passage that clefts the bosom of this land, and to the north, where the waters beneath us flow together and commingle with the arctic seas.

Behind me I hear the drumming and the mournful wail of the singers offering up their final song.

It is good, I tell myself, to live in this land of transitions, this land incipient with change, where the heart is drawn always beyond itself, and every ending is numinous with hope.

THE RED EARTH

The Red Dirt Ennobled Their Faces

Jim Klobuchar

I don't remember his face, but I do remember his forearms. They were big and hairy and they separated me from three of my best front teeth in a high school football game in northern Minnesota nearly thirty-five years ago.

He's a Minneapolis businessman now. Because our tracks carry us in different directions, we haven't met for years. He telephoned on the pretense of talking about the election. The discussion was perfunctory and not especially profound. He drifted through this and that for a few minutes, and then confided that his father died a few weeks ago. He wasn't morose about it. His father was an iron miner who lived into his eighties. He was a pensioner who seemed comfortable in the last years of his life, satisfied materially and lifted by the knowledge that his kids had achieved and were well off.

The son was groping for a response to his father's death beyond the natural grief that had subsided. He asked what he could do in memory of his father's sacrifices for his family as an immigrant iron miner.

I never met the one he called "the old man," but I knew hundreds like him. They were my relatives, my neighbors, and my gruff tutors when I was a kid. To earn money for school, I shoveled iron ore at their sides in the dripping red tunnels of the underground mines. At lunchtime in the little wood shack fifteen hundred feet beneath the surface, they would rummage through their lunch pails, wrap their ore-smeared hands around a pork chop sandwich, and talk. Some of them were vulgar and a few were silly, and their giggling voices gave me an odd kind of shiver, as though a colony of comics had been turned loose in a tomb. They spoke in broken English or in their native Yugoslavian, Finnish, or Italian. The collision of their languages heightened the alien vibrations in the shack.

It was a place where I saw my first pornographic pictures, and where I first learned something about beauty.

Most of the men ate without speaking. Some of them chewed absently, some reflectively. They worked in grime and never very far from the threat of caving earth. They were human moles. When poets celebrated the dignity of man, they might not have been thinking very hard about underground miners. Their faces were smudged from rubbing the rock wall when they set a drill bit or a dynamite stick. The seams in their faces were streaked with ore dirt. They had the caricature look of actors painted by a deranged makeup artist who ignored the rims of white skin under their mining helmets and lathered the rest in red.

But they didn't make the sounds or strike the postures of martyred men. They and their wives came of their own accord. Nobody would erect any monuments to their fame or their work, but there was something deeper that absorbed them. One of the miners wore a long, coffee-strain mustache in the old-country style. His black eyes roamed the walls fiercely enough to split the ore unaided. But he motioned for me to come to his bench, and he talked about his son and the "big university." The glare vanished, and he shook his head in wonderment. *His kid,* going to the big university.

People ask now and then what to see if they visit the ore towns of northern Minnesota. I tell them to look in on the museums and the abandoned pits, but to find a place, a barbershop or a saloon or maybe a lodge hall, where they can look into the faces and hear the voices of another and earlier America now almost gone.

The immigrants still come to this country. But the ones I remember came at a time when the hungers of their ambition for their children fused with the restless yearnings of the young country and produced something marvelous. It was a country that demanded and abused, inspired and rewarded. It did all of those things to the immigrants I remember. But before they worked their last they engraved for us a truth: that much of this country's greatness springs from the struggles of its people, the ones it first exploited, and then needed.

That their children recognize it is their best memorial.

Dear Folks

Matthew Miltich

Our Old Man told us to say we were Austrian, if asked at school, and it was true that on Grampa's immigration papers his country of origin was listed as Austria-Hungary. When I told Sister Marita in fourth grade that I was Australian, she gave me a penetrating look and said that didn't seem possible, I must be mistaken. All I truly knew about our ethnicity was that there seemed some essential difference between our own tribe of happily wild children and the other kids in Grand Rapids during the middle and late 1950s. Dad's people came from Europe, but by way of the Iron Range.

From the top of any of the big pines in our town you'd have been able to see the mine dumps. But beginning just five miles east of our town, the character of the towns strung like rusty beads along Highway 169 to Virginia, Minnesota, where Grampa and Gramma lived, was different from Grand Rapids. In those towns the streets were narrow, houses only a human wingspan apart along the crowded blocks, backyards just five jumps across. In the narrow alleys behind their houses, according to my Old Man, immigrants had bought grapes shipped from California every summer in semi trucks to make their wine.

Across the Range red rock was tumbled in broken heaps as big as mountains, every side road made a red track, and every light-colored car or truck glowed dirty pink. Even the houses in its towns stood behind a film of pinkish dust.

But if the streets were narrower they were also more intimate than the wide streets of our town, with corner grocery stores and little shops with interesting-sounding family names on their signs. It seemed that the Old Man knew the nationality of everyone's name and always remarked about it and knew even the real name behind the Anglicized version of names used now.

When we passed the graveyard in Hibbing, its tiny American flags standing over the war veterans buried there, he'd talk about Uncle Steve, dead many years and buried here, a glider pilot during the war, who as a boy ski-jumped off the mine dumps and once walked the high wire and swung on the trapeze for a circus. He'd changed his name to Miller. Even our own family name had somehow lost the *e* in the middle, gone from Miletich to Miltich. Uncle Tony, a surgeon, pronounced it *mil-tick,* to sound German. Once in Grampa and Gramma's kitchen in Virginia I asked Dad what our name meant. "Dear," he said. And that was neat, I thought, to have a name that meant "deer," the most beautiful and graceful of all God's creatures. Dad straightened me out, but I still liked it.

Any trip across the Iron Range to Grampa and Gramma's meant a stop at Aunt Anna Mae's in Eveleth. Anna Mae was Dad's sister. When you first arrived, Aunt Anna Mae would fold you into her arms as her face dissolved in tears. This happened every time. She had a way of holding you at arm's length just before she pulled you close, love and compassion in her eyes melting all at once to tears as she folded you to her breast. This was *not* uncomfortable or strange. Her voice repeating your name two or three times as she held you was assurance you were loved and understood, your sorrows and triumphs hers as well. And seconds later you were re-leased while she wiped her tears away with her fine, long fingers, and now her smile and no trace of sorrow.

Anna Mae and Uncle John ran a corner store that smelled of homemade sausage and fresh meat and vegetables. The floor was maple, the meat case white enameled steel with a shining glass window. A bubble gum machine with its glass globe filled with big colored gumballs stood at the front of the store near the cash regis-ter. That was the only machine the Old Man ever let me put a coin into, the only bubble gum he ever gave the okay for. Anna Mae and her family lived in the same building with the store, which seemed rare and wonderful to me.

But it was the house in Virginia and its two old dwellers that were most compelling to me. Grampa and Gramma's kitchen was white—counter, cupboards, and table—and in winter seemed whiter than the snow. Stew always simmered in a sunken pot, a new piece of meat or vegetable added each day, but the original stock seeming to go all the way back to when Dad was a boy. To my tongue it was delicious beyond description and not like any-thing regular Americans ate.

The kitchen and the basement were the places in the house that felt lived in. Grampa still drank his own wine at every meal but breakfast, and in his basement were the tools of his wine making: a wine press, hundred-gallon wooden casks, bottles, a sink and counter. In Grampa's basement I smelled my first cigar smoke, took my first swallow of his zinfandel, sat with him and listened to stories about the old country.

"The old country" was a phrase used dozens of times on every visit to Grampa and Gramma's, spoken by Gramma and Grampa and by my Old Man, too. While I sat with Grampa in the basement Dad would talk upstairs with Gramma, or when the three of them would sit together at the white table in the kitchen I'd wander in the house, hearing from the kitchen a mix of English and the lan-guage from the old country. Frequently from my father a question:

"Kako po nashu?"—How in ours? How do we say it in our language? In that house for me "the old country" was an imagined place, a seacoast, I understood, and rocky, a place where it never snowed, where the people, who were my people, spoke in that strange language that by now was familiar but of which I could understand only a few words and phrases here and there, while the meanings I could not catch spilled out in a torrent, faster than I could listen.

It was strange, too, to wander in the house to look at photographs of people, even of the aunts and uncles I knew, who looked American now, with grave eyes and faces, in clothing from a lost past. The upstairs rooms still held their beds and chests of drawers. On the walls with their photographs were crucifixes and holy cards or bits of palm frond woven into a cross from a long passed Palm Sunday. Ten children had lived in the house, but now these rooms, though furnished, seemed vacant. A chime clock on the buffet in the dining room tick-tocked the seconds and chimed the hours and half-hours. Its steady, relentless sound made the quiet in the house larger.

In the cloakroom, a kind of anteroom just off the dining room, Grampa and Gramma had hung their wedding picture, a picture of the whole family together, and pictures of relatives from the old country or scattered across the earth. From every face stared those grave, trenchant eyes.

Like the house, Grampa and Gramma held their histories in themselves. Gramma was as kind as Aunt Anna Mae and as tender of touch, but in place of Anna Mae's tears and smiles Gramma accepted my kiss with resignation, as she accepted everything, it seemed to me. Her eyes were blue, her hair fine and white, and even to my young touch she felt frail. Her English was broken and difficult to understand, but even so, my aunt Katherine had told me, she forbid her own children to speak the old language at home when they were little. My father told me that in the old country when she was a girl no girl children were taught to read and write, only how to work in the home and fields. To me she spoke never an unkind word, but I never saw her smile.

Grampa's English was as broken as Gramma's, but his spirit was not. If Gramma accepted all things with resignation, Grampa scorned and repudiated the world's measurement of things, preferring his own. You could see it in the set of his lips and eyebrows and the way he held his head, his lifted jaw. He still raged against the injustices of the old country, the years in the open pit mines, the men who judged him fit only for brute labor, who promised a mild climate like the old country but sent him to the mines in northern Minnesota where he was greeted by thirty below zero when he climbed off the train. He'd stowed away on a boat, my Old Man told me, to get away from being drafted by the Austrians.

If his English was broken, he'd made it his own language, spoke it with authority and passion and cursed as fluently and freely as any Yank or Britisher. My Old Man told him to watch it in front of his boys, but Grampa laughed. If a story or a man deserved a curse, Grampa cursed.

My father was tall and broad-shouldered and quick to anger, but despite losing his temper often enough, it seemed, he was, under it all, as gentle and sensitive as Gramma. But Grampa was genuinely fierce, and frightening to a boy small as myself. Dad said that when he was a kid if the Old Man came home drunk, he and his brothers would push the chest of drawers and bed against the bedroom door to keep him out, he was that frightening. He showed me Grampa's razor strop in the bathroom, a heavy, broad leather belt. Misbehave, and he'd use the razor strop on you, my Old Man said.

Yet when I was with him Grampa was mirthful. Even in his old age he was powerful, with great wide shoulders and tremendous arms. They called him Big Andy in the mines, he told me, and no one ever beat him in arm wrestling. Once he and a big Swede went at it for hours, he said, in Hibbing, neither man able to put the other's arm down. But never beaten, he said. Yet his hands were beautiful, as if sculpted, unmarked by his boyhood and youth fishing the Adriatic or by a lifetime in the pits, and with those hands he'd hold my head or touch my face, then laugh and laugh.

Sometimes his laughter was sardonic or black, but mostly, it seemed to me, he was simply amused. The world, as he grew older, seemed a sillier and sillier place as people forgot the lessons of both old country and new. The radio and television were full of nonsense, and he attended only what deserved his attention, the making of wine, the preparing and eating of food, the cultivating and harvesting of his garden. The backyard of the house in Virginia was narrow and small, but Grampa gardened it intensely. Most of dinner or supper in summer came right out of the backyard.

It was by Grampa and Gramma's example that I came to understand that food itself is sacramental, to be prayed over, savored, taken in gratitude, eaten slowly and with decorum. Grampa and Gramma held their forks and knives differently from the way my mother instructed us at home, but in their hands they seemed used rightly. They used bread as a utensil, dipping it in their food, cleaning their plates. When the meal was finished, the plates glowed as if washed. Starvation, Grampa and Gramma gave me to understand, was something they knew firsthand in the old country.

At their table Grampa served me coffee. My father suggested it might stunt my growth, to which Grampa replied by forcing a short burst of air through his lips—a voiceless sound he used to dismiss anything he deemed nonsense. "Drink em bleck," he said to me, "mek you man." Bitter and awful it tasted, but I drank every drop. He served me red wine, too, cut with a little water in a small glass. Both Gramma and Dad disapproved. "*Malo*. Just a little won't hurt him," Grampa said.

At that table I could imagine my father's whole family gathered for a meal as children. My father described a winter night, black as death outside the windows, everyone hungry, the littlest kids at table, the older girls helping Gramma, Grampa just home from the pit, stripped to the waist, the fierce cold already making frost patterns on the windows, steam from the potatoes. Grampa stands at the sink, his face, his hair, his chest, his back stained red with ore dust, everything quiet while they wait for him to wash. He turns to the children. "Look at me," he says. He shows them the upturned palms of his hands, his fingers spread. "Is this what you want? Work in the pit? Don't go to school," he says, "this is what you get."

Just across the street from the house in Virginia was the grade school the children attended. The houses on Grampa and Gramma's side were hard by the street and hard by each other, but the school yard was wide and open. Dad told us about the slide from the upper stories used in fire drills, about how the youngest kids came to school unable to speak English. It was in the public schools that my aunts and uncles learned impeccable English. Uncle Paul, speaking only the old country tongue when first sent to school, would become press secretary to the vice president of the United States. In the school, my father and his brothers learned to read music. My father could read an orchestral score and hear every note of it in his head. He spoke of his high school music teacher, Vernon Malone, as a patron saint who kept him in school and finally encouraged him to attend junior college and then university to take a degree in music.

My Old Man would point out the houses of his boyhood friends and of folks he knew when he was small. Across those yards and in them he played and learned bits and pieces, the syntax of the Indo-European languages he heard and especially the music of English spoken with the inflections and intonations of whatever tongue had come first. He repeated the words just as he heard them when he was a boy, played with the sounds of languages as a jazzman plays with notes.

On the streets and in the shops of Virginia he'd greet people in their own tongues. When he stopped to visit with some friend or acquaintance, he'd talk at length, European-style, and whether shop or street corner, summer or winter, I'd have to wait a long time before we could go along our way.

After a long day at Grampa and Gramma's I'd kiss them good-bye, a good combination of old man smell and wine from Grampa, his face rough with the day's whiskers, thick black hairs growing right out of his ears, Gramma's kiss tender and sad. Then out to the car, the inside dials lighting up as the Old Man turned on the headlights and drove out to the highway. Seeming lighter now, he would turn on the radio. He knew every tune, all the lyrics, and tapped his wedding ring in time on the steering wheel.

The two-lane highway wound in and out of every little town, all mining towns, the yards and houses like Grampa and Gramma's, red mine dumps for backdrop, aspen suckers trying to reclaim their talus slopes for life again. I'd stretch out on the wide front seat of the Ford and put my head in Dad's lap and listen to the music and his stories. Sometimes I'd begin to drift, the pale light from the dials fading as I fell asleep. Come morning I'd wake in the room at home with my brothers.

We weren't Austrian, that was sure, if Grampa ran away from being drafted by the Austrians. And the old language Grampa and Gramma spoke, Grampa called *Hrvatski*, Croatian, so we were Croatian, our Old Man finally admitted to us. But there was old, bad blood between the Croatians and the Serbians, he said, and bad trouble during the Second World War between Croatian nationalists and Serbs and others besides, and on the Iron Range, he told us, the Serbs, the Slovenes, the Croats all called themselves Yugoslavs, the south Slavs, but really, he said, we were Dalmatian. I knew I could never say at school that I was Dalmatian; the kids would tease.

They had gone back to Dalmatia, Dad said, when he was nine. Grampa, he said, never meant to leave the old country for good. Gramma was against going back. She wanted to stay in the new country, where even the poor didn't starve. But they went, all but Katherine, who went to stay with Uncle Peter in Spokane. They went by steamship. Dad remembered the dolphins that leapt in front of the ship. He remembered Grampa's village. "They had nothing," he said. "Only the sea. The sea was their garden." He remembered stealing grapes with his cousins.

Grampa wanted to build a hotel, he said. But there were thieves. And government corruption. The family left Grampa's village and went to Gramma's village.

Dad remembered the old stone house there, the well and bucket outside, the stable, an outdoor oven for baking bread, olive trees seen from the bedroom window. He remembered a pretty girl named Kate in the village. He remembered an instrument played like a fiddle, how he learned to play. Once, he said, his old man took him to the ancient walled city of Dubrovnik and bought him a steak in a restaurant. Finally, after a year, money all gone and no prospects, they took the steamship back to America, the trains back to Virginia, Minnesota, Grampa back to the iron mines.

Gramma died in winter. I was just starting high school then. My Old Man and I arrived at the house in Virginia one day and found Grampa alone in the kitchen. Gramma, he said, had decided to die. She was upstairs in bed and wouldn't take food. We found her up there. A glass of milk was going bad on the chest of drawers. Just as Grampa said, she told Dad it was time for her to die. To me she looked as old as a person can get, frail as a nestling in her bed, peaceful and resigned.

There's nothing you can do, Grampa told us. But no, Dad said. He called an ambulance, and men came, unloaded a stretcher, came into the house and up the stairs to get Gramma. I remember them carrying her down the stairs and out through the porch and front door. She drew her old hand in from where it grasped the side rail just in time to avoid having it crushed in the door frame.

In the hospital Dad left me by her side as she lay in her hospital bed. I gave her tiny sips of ice water by dipping a straw into a glass, capping the open end with my finger, then lifting the finger to let the water run into her mouth. I held her hand and she looked helplessly into my eyes.

Late in the afternoon, Dad cut Grampa's hair in the kitchen of the old house. "Before I married her," Grampa told him, "I wondered if she was strong enough."

"No, Pa," Dad said. "Don't say that." Grampa shrugged.

"No matter now," Grampa said.

On the day we buried her, snow began to fall in the cemetery in Virginia. The trees were gray, the ground frozen and snow-covered. My brothers, sisters, and I, all but the youngest two, who stayed home with neighbors, began to cry as Gramma's coffin was lowered into the earth. Our aunts and uncles stood with us, grim and silent, and there were cousins in the cemetery with us too, but it was my brothers and sisters and I who wept. As I felt the tears run on my cold cheeks, I knew it was not for Gramma's death that I wept, but for her life.

I love my country. That is, I love the smell of wild plum blossoms every spring and the calls of loons; I love to hear the ripping sounds the ring-necked ducks make in the fall when they tear the sky with their wings; I love the first fall of snow in northern Minnesota and the way the light lies on the land in December, for this is the place of my nativity, but I understood something about Gramma when I walked with my father up the long road from Slano to Grbljava and the little village of Rajkovici in Croatia where Gramma was born.

My Old Man took me with him, God bless him and rest him, when he went back to the old country for the last time. The road was steep, but at its end stood the house where he lived that year he was nine years old. To me, every step along the dusty road up the hills from the sea felt remembered, though I'd never been anywhere even remotely like this before. I remembered it from the stories. This was the old country of my imagination, the place I dreamed as I listened to Gramma and Grampa and Dad in the kitchen in Virginia.

Here was the imagined house, built all of stone, the old stable, the well, the olive trees. Here was my Old Man's cousin, who still lived in the house, grown old now, his daughters and their families, my relatives. Here was food and wine and tears and a feeling like a thunderstorm in my chest that here at last were the rest of my people, longed for and dreamed about, so that I felt more welcomed and home, right there in that strange, foreign land, than I'd ever felt in the town where I was born.

It was then I thought I knew something about Gramma I hadn't understood before. To leave this place, to lose it, that was the sorrow, I thought, that clouded her heart. To lose not only the mild air and the smell of wild thyme and rosemary and lavender, the hills and the blue Adriatic below, the stone houses, the vineyards and orchards, but the people too, the language, the food, this was to lose almost everything, an entire life. I could see in the land its own history, soil thin and dry, everywhere rock, orchards and vineyards growing only where stone walls protected the little soil, every rock set by hand. I asked Ivo, the old cousin, about the walls. "You don't go out and build a wall," Ivo said. "When you walk along the road, you pick up a stone. You put the stone in the wall. In this way, after five hundred years you have a wall."

Here the land had been parceled and reparceled, in each generation the land going to the eldest son. For the others, less and less remained. For Gramma there was nothing. There was no place to go but away. From a land of sunshine and a crystal sea, stone palaces and walled cities, she came to rest finally in Minnesota's Iron Range. The day of her funeral, the snow that began to fall in the morning became a blizzard. After taking Uncle Tony to the airport in Duluth, we drove home in the dark through a roaring wind and snow so thick we could hardly find our way.

My favorite memory of Grampa is me wrapped in his arms in his bed at the cabin on Lake Fourteen. I was a little boy alone with the old man for a week's fishing in early summer in a cabin with no electric lights or running water, and no heat. The first night I was afraid to sleep with him. "Cold night," Grampa said, "you sleep with me." But I stubbornly kept to my own small bunk in a corner of the dark cabin till I woke up freezing. I could hear him sleeping in the darkness across the cabin, a heavy intake of breath, a burst of air through his lips as he exhaled. Freezing in my little-kid pajamas, I found his bed in the dark by the sound of his breathing, woke him, and asked if I could come in. He opened his bed and pulled me in, laughing; then my head was against the rough hair on his chest, and the heat of his body quieted my shivering, and I fell right to sleep while he laughed.

The village of his birth, Miletici, is north of Zadar on the sea. The coastal hills rise barren and rocky above it. Everywhere lie stones. In a little stone house Dad and I found Anna Benic, Grampa's sister, Grampa's very face in her own. She was an old woman, but her sons lived in the village too. In their faces and their bare chests, burned brown by Dalmatian sunshine, I saw my own father, my uncles, my brothers. Poor. So poor they seemed to own only the stones themselves, but here also was food and wine. Anna's old husband offered us wine. It was morning, but sunny and dry and already hot and no shade anywhere but inside the house. I asked for water. Nikola, the old man, tall and spare and white haired, laughed. "Water is for women and children," he said. I said, "Surely you drink water." He pulled himself straight, his shoulders back and chin up. "I haven't had a drink of water in fifty years," he said.

Strong people, the people of Miletici, and proud and stubborn, the men tall and barrel chested, the women stout and sturdy. In my father's cousins I saw Grampa's sharp eye and the tilt of his head. There too I was embraced by my family. One old man in the village told me that long ago his father went to America and never returned. "When I was a boy, whenever I thought of him," he said, "my heart skipped like a lamb," and he twirled his cane to show how light he felt.

Grampa lived to be ninety-three, many years beyond Gramma. The day of his funeral was the hottest day of that year. Five of my brothers and I bore his coffin. The church isn't far from the old house in Virginia, but Grampa hadn't lived in the house for years. After the funeral I walked alone from the church and found the old house. The corner store at the foot of the hill was closed and boarded up. The elementary school across from Gramma and Grampa's house was boarded up, too. I walked through the narrow alleyway. The little backyard was grassed over. No trace of Grampa's garden remained.

But in the hot glare of that July noon, I remembered the garden, and I remembered something more: flowers. Every spring and summer while Grampa and Gramma lived there, the yard was alive with the color of flowers, just as in Croatia—in window boxes, flowerpots and gardens, in the poorest house and the richest dwelling, flowers everywhere.

Though their families were poor and struggled to make a living, Grampa and Gramma were more than just simple peasants. They were descended from one of the oldest peoples in Europe, with a distinct culture, their own dances, foods, celebrations, who brought one of the first organized kingdoms to south central Europe. Grampa and Gramma knew who they were.

But like many of our people, Grampa and Gramma were forced to choose between a foredoomed struggle to hold fast to their rocky birthplace or to sail away into the wide world in hope of finding a place where they could make a life for themselves. In the new country they found each other, and, the dear folks, they did the best they could.

From the top of the tallest tree on our farmstead you can see the mine dumps, and some of the neighbors still go off to work in the mines. The road across the Range between our house and Grampa and Gramma's linked my family and me not just with another household, but with our people. Grampa and Gramma never tried to teach us Croatian culture and history. They simply passed on to us the old, true things that any people must pass along to keep the people whole. When I remember Gramma and Grampa, our relatives across the ocean, and my own dear Old Man, my father, I still ache with loss. But I love to walk across our land here, over the pasture and hay fields and along the lanes. When I find a stone pushing up through the earth, I carry it to the wall, growing stone by stone, along our north field.

Next Wilderness

Steven R. Downing

I'm looking here at a landscape of mine dumps, discard mounds, overburden, at the very western end of northern Minnesota's Mesabi Range. (*Mesabi*—sleeping giant, the Ojibwe named the red hills, and they didn't have to translate it for us.) The iron ore streak ran out in this place, a hundred-plus miles southwest of where it started, and the land looks it, looks run out. If that's what it is.

From the top of these purple-orange discard mounds you take in a vista blown open and picked over; the lassitude, earth's faintness, is physical, is yours. You breathe it, smell it, the smell of iron and blood. But the only thing dead or dying here is an idea, a human conceit: the notion that things are what they are strictly because our human needs and hopes require them to be just that. The teleological approach.

A hundred-plus years ago gold actually appeared to lie under this commonplace cover of woods, wetlands, rolling hills. In that dream of gold sensible people risked everything they had, and much that they didn't have, on whatever heroics were called for in exploding away the Mesabi's quartzite surface (really a mutant sandstone). Below, in anything the earth would give up, the rewards had to emerge, had to. Smelling blood, finding no gold, these groundbreakers ground down through the several recoverable layers of magnetite and hematite. Iron ore mining. The open pit method, they eventually called it, with an ear tin-deaf to irony. More often than not they had to settle for sandy low-grade ore, usable only when the eastern blast furnaces were refusing nothing, back when producing a ton of steel was both a moral and a capital responsibility. There were two world wars to win or lose. Never mind that it might take two tons of iron to produce a ton of steel.

They didn't know it at the time, but these early miners were digging in two directions at once; backward in time to the Cretaceous, and ahead, to some future Cretaceous. A next generation of dinosaurs will plausibly wade and reproduce and perish in mine dump lakes, deep machine-round lakes created in this land by Andrew Carnegie, John Rockefeller, Chester Congdon, J. P. Morgan.

I'm looking here at this still vaguely Cretaceous landscape, at what grows on the dumps now: birch and aspen mainly. Spindly aspen, growing either in dense impenetrable thickets or one cartoony tree every thousand feet, up from roots like steel wire. Spindly birch, seemingly without the energy to make branches and leaves. The impression is of bones, shinbones and thighbones especially, stuck on end into the purple-orange hills. Hills geometrically graded and flat-topped as though emptied from giant sand pails. Some are only large enough to accommodate beer parties. Some could hold whole towns. They do look ready for that next Pleistocene day when we'll be picking through the rocks once more, picking and settling for reductions of ore somewhat finer than our ancestors settled for.

Our immigrant ancestors had no second thoughts in this business of iron mining. Life was day-to-day ungracious for them, and they moved without reflection from one pressing need to the next. Many of them lived to see the streak run out. Two generations and it was all over at this end of the Mesabi. If they noticed any disagreement between what things were and what things should have been they called it an act of God and kept on with it.

Now the land in this place looks somehow benignly bombed: a debris-scape, yes, but there's no sense of anything particularly valuable gone. The sleeping giant rolled over. What's next? The woods are trying to reclaim the land, though at this geologic moment the birch are dying and the aspen appear moribund, not only where the mines were but where the forests around the mines were. The sentiment is easy, no doubt too easy: things went too far here.

In the early 1970s this manner of thinking prompted a more hands-on approach to land reclamation, born of impatience with the new scratch forest's laissez-faire comeback. Earth Day, as concept and tactic, had the whiff of something selfless and hip; it could not fail. High schools began offering classes in earth science under the headings *The Environment and You. Eco-Biology. Chemistry for Tree-Huggers.* As class projects, students did things like plant Christmas trees on some of the local discard mounds. These Christmas tree saplings were all uniform in height and girth and needle formation. Uniform still, the Christmas trees stand up and down the purple-orange hills now in rows so straight, in two directions, the process of natural erosion is occurring at precisely right angles. A predictable story, so no one predicted it. Whole artsy parcels of the Christmas tree dumps have turned perfectly orange, a story no one has to tell anyone.

Our storytelling, since Darwin, has proclaimed that as humans we've finally prevailed over all things, and against all bets, in some long-running planetary free-for-all. Everything was an advancement of our purpose. If there was iron under this ground, it must have been put there for us to mine. The Ojibwe we treated into kindnesses we never deserved thought they were handing over only a shovel's depth of all this ground, for planting. Who's to blame for our dreaming and digging deep enough to find iron ore? Soon enough we learned how to split the atom and then learned subsequent lessons about our own divisible power and steel-making dreams. And even then, the inexhaustible iron ore was about gone, like the inexhaustible white pine before it. Talk about dreams.

In one sense we now have the freedom to make decisions in a new way, decisions about mining and cutting trees, say. New categories and visions of waste, of use, new choices. In another sense we find it paralyzing. Who knows what's coming, anymore? Or wants to, is the thing. Since you never know, you probably shouldn't. That is, why not choose to regard a bone-tree-topped mine dump as an aesthetic and economic triumph, something well finished? Then choose to leave it as it is.

As it is today, the bell sky overhead is a deep 3-D blue—no smog or mist or scrimmy haze between the Mesabi and the Van Allen belts at the moment. The uncommonly purple-orange discard mounds, massed and isolated so weirdly, ranging in content from sharp-edged fist-sized chunks to immense smooth boulders, all absorb the sunlight absolutely. There's no glint, no compromising hint of about-to-be-steel, on these opaque hills. Ruddy, but dull. And to call the white woods here failed is to miss the point. Maybe they're just the new look in trees. Cool actually, trees so white and uncluttered and upreaching. What the trees are so flimsily but unrelentingly anchored in—who knows what that crustal sediment of inverted glacial drift and human leftovers will cook up next?

And humans still do use this place year round, on foot, on skis, snowmobiles, all-terrain vehicles, bikes. Here, they're out of town, out of their neighbors' hair, closer to something halfway mysterious, halfway risky. Back in the 1960s, local storytellers decided this was the safest place to jazz up a mescaline or mushroom or some such high, to inflate it with possibility. Safe, in that you weren't likely to hurt yourself or anyone else out here. Jazzy, in that you could count on the entertainment value of a trippy improvising wander among the ruins and rocks. A ghostly terrain, so there were ghosts. Ghosts, and no one materially there to shake you down for making too much of it all, with all that noise. Today, you can speak openly of those times. You're so old, finally, you can get away with it.

You see white-tailed deer out here now, and partridge, black bears. Skunks, porcupines. Raccoons. The beavers are back, working the wet spots of ex-mine and ex-forest. Red and gray squirrels, rabbits, bald eagles, red-tailed and rough-legged hawks, woodchucks, circling yapping cleanup ravens . . . all seem obliviously at home in this environment. Never mind that human economists and aesthetes alike might call it an unmitigated disaster area.

Here, on the westernmost Mesabi, I'm alone at the moment on this standout purple-orange discard mound. The still air itself seems blue—really almost a particulate blueness. And the woods, all white. From here, looking north, you can see the Mississippi River, flowing eastward yet at this point, defying here the gravity of both Hudson Bay and the Gulf of Mexico. This northward down-curving vista includes the continental divide, and what you have to suppose is Canadian sky. All over. This is it.

What It Means to Be an American in Coleraine, Minnesota

Sharon Miltich

We grew up knowing that our pristine town on Minnesota's Mesabi Iron Range had connections to the presidency. Founded by John C. Greenway, former Rough Rider and a friend to Theodore Roosevelt, Coleraine has always been as American as the eagles that still nest in the pine trees out on the peninsula across Trout Lake.

We have a large red, white, and blue flag made of painted rocks dug into the green hillside overlooking Longyear Park. Until recent years, we had a four-day celebration in honor of Independence Day. Those who lived in Coleraine and those who—like me—called it home because we went to school, church, ball games, and dances there, shared the belief that towns like ours were what America should be made of. We were the adopted daughters and sons of the mining baron Greenway; the grand-nieces and -nephews, we liked to think, of Teddy Roosevelt himself.

For us, Greenway built a model village along the shore of Trout Lake at the western edge of America's richest iron mining range. He and the town fathers built a high school complete with marble steps, oil paintings, and chandeliers; a lush city park with curving walkways and intricate Victorian gardens; a swimming beach; a band shell and a dance pavilion. He laid out Lakeview Boulevard along the shore of Trout Lake and lined it with rows of colonial homes—each one different from the others—for mine workers and their families.

To be from Coleraine, Minnesota, in the 1960s was to know that John Greenway, the friend of a president, was watching. It's no wonder my little-girl image of God was neither bearded nor robed in white. No, God was a distinguished, gray-haired gentleman in a business suit and glasses. In my mind, God looked just like all the pictures I'd seen of Mr. John C. Greenway.

1963. Mrs. Peters asks every child whose mother attended the PTA meeting last night to stand. She marches up and down the five straight rows of third graders, focusing not on those of us who have risen, but on the four or five students who remain in their desks. "Tut tut," she says softly, shaking her head. She begins to put stars on the foreheads of the PTA mothers' children.

Just as Mrs. Peters prepares to place my star, Miss Lameroux, our blue-haired librarian, knocks on the classroom door. Our teacher steps into the hall and pulls the door closed behind her. I notice through the long rectangle of glass that Miss Lameroux is crying. Mrs. Peters stands nervously, right hand on the doorknob, glancing in at us every few seconds. She fidgets with the white handkerchief tucked under the belt of her dark blue dress before she opens the door and walks solemnly to the front of the room. She takes one deep breath, looks us over.

"Boys and girls, your president has been shot."

I stare blankly out the window, past the steel-gray waters of Trout Lake to Longyear Park. I fix my gaze on the painted-rock flag until the sniffling and shuffling of other students pull me back inside the classroom. On the window ledge are rows of plastic bags filled with taconite pellets. Neatly labeled and packaged, they were donated by U.S. Steel. We are learning about taconite, a low-grade, processed ore. Taconite, we've been told, is our future. I stare at the brownish-red rocks.

Finally, Mrs. Peters speaks. "What is this country coming to," she says, her question flattened into a statement. Then, after a long silence, "Don't be surprised if the Russians use this moment of weakness to attack us." We stare at her, wide-eyed. "Duck your heads when you leave here today," she adds later. "Get home quickly and stay there, because anything could happen."

Mrs. Peters removes her handkerchief from her belt and uses it to dab at her eyes. "Anything could happen," she repeats softly, looking out over the surface of the lake as if scanning for submarines. "Even here . . . especially here." Her energy and volume are returning. "Here in the heart of America . . . here in Coleraine, Minnesota . . . are the kind of people . . . the Communists . . . fear." Mrs. Peters alternately whispers, shouts, and pauses, presenting each word and each part of a word as a separate, vital truth. She smacks the palm of her hand against the top of her oak desk to accentuate the stronger truths. "*Here* . . . are the *people* . . . who *know* . . . what it *is* . . . to *be* . . . an . . . AMERICAN." Both hands hit the desktop at her final word. I jump, then slump down in my desk.

When the intercom crackles and Principal Brennan announces that school will be let out early, we line up in the school's front hallway near a portrait of Mr. Greenway. We wait our turn to be led down through the concrete tunnel between the grade school and the high school parking lot. Mrs. Peters blows her pitch pipe and leads us in her shaky soprano through three verses of "The Star-Spangled Banner."

A slow procession of bright orange buses assembles along the parking lot curb. My bus is always the first in line—boarding to rural Trout Lake, LaPrairie, the River Road. It leaves the parking lot and makes a sharp left turn, gears groaning, past the yellow-bricked Carnegie library. As we make our way toward Roosevelt Avenue I see mothers on sidewalks and in alleyways, waiting for their children. The library flag already hangs at half-mast as housewives, in cotton dresses and aprons, gather in twos and threes under the elm trees along the boulevard.

1972. It is the summer of the Watergate break-in and my father keeps saying that America as he knows it is dead. He's a Republican—and to be one of those on the Mesabi Range means you're willing to stand alone. Dad doesn't seem to mind; he's been an outsider ever since he and Mom moved north from Iowa fifteen years ago and built our place a few miles from Coleraine.

Dad started out working in the mines, handling a broom, washing down machinery like a lot of other young guys. He quit after six months—took a big pay cut to work twice as hard peeling logs in the pulp room at the paper mill in Grand Rapids. Security was the reason, he said, security and common sense.

"The mines are on their way out," he'd tell us. "You can't keep digging dirt out of the ground without putting anything back." He liked to drive past the paper mill's tree nurseries on Sundays, to show us that the paper company plants more timber than it cuts down. Still, it was hard on Dad to leave the mines, even after only six months; harder still to leave the paper mill when numbness and tingling took over one side of his body and turned into multiple sclerosis. When layoffs and shutdowns crept like a cancer through Coleraine and the rest of the Range, it was hard on him to be right—and hard now to have been so wrong about Richard Nixon.

His paper mill, his politics, his wife and daughters. Dad's loyalties are cut and dried like the timber he scraped and sawed and piled. So when he sits at the table after dinner, holding a coffee cup in hands from which stiff fingers splay out like spikes on a spider plant, and announces that America's sprung a leak, he expects our full attention. Instead, Mom washes dishes while my sisters argue over whose turn it will be to mow the lawn tomorrow, and whether the chores have to be completely finished before Mom will let us sun ourselves in the backyard or ride our bikes to the Coleraine beach.

As for me, I watch the sun set outside the dining room window and open the fresh, clean pages of a book of poems by Sara Teasdale. "Happy Seventeenth Birthday," Mom has written inside the front cover. "May life be full of poetry, love, and laughter."

Oh, to be Sara Teasdale, I think. Dark hair, dark eyes, writer of pretty words like these, loved (according to the biographical note) by a poet named Vachel Lindsay. A name like Sara has a cleanness to it: simplicity, delicacy, grace. But according to my Iowa relatives, I am "a sturdy German girl," brown-haired, big-boned, with "hands made for work and hips for having babies."

"Mickey," Mom says, "I'm done washing. Your turn to dry and put away." After dishes she and I walk half a mile down the road to see if the blackberries are ripe in the ditches along the Jensens' weedy pasture. The Jensens' house is too small for a family with five boys, so the older ones sleep in a bunkhouse out back. They walk around in white undershirts and none of them pick blackberries, so we are welcome to them. On our way home with a half-bucket of dust-covered berries I see Robert, the youngest at seventeen, sitting on the Jensens' front steps. James Dean with red hair and a black Fender guitar, he picks out the first line to "House of the Rising Sun" over and over until he gets it right. Robert nods at me as we walk past, then looks back down at his awkward fingers.

My friend Barb and I leave her big house on Roosevelt Avenue the last Friday night in August. We haven't said for sure that we'll go to the party at the abandoned airstrip up near the pit, but we know that's where we'll end up. Twelfth grade social life revolves around keggers. It's high time we appeared on the scene. We cross the manicured green lawn of Longyear Park and follow the wooded path around Trout Lake. Just before we reach the peninsula we turn right onto the old mine road and hike past a spot where town kids skinny dip on moonlit nights. We have arrived.

David Petrovich, our soon-to-be senior class president, looks over at me from the other side of a blazing bonfire. Barb brings me a beer. "What's a nice girl like you doing here?" he calls out. David's voice is big like the noisy booms that shake Coleraine each morning and night as miners blast deeper into the disappearing red rock of the pit at the edge of town. His laugh is loud but slow and steady, like the aftershocks that rock the ground under our feet as if we are babies and the earth is our cradle.

"What's a nice boy like you," I say back.

They call David "Dutch" because, of course, he's Yugoslav. The nicknames we give each other provide Coleraine's English teachers with their only shred of hope that we are absorbing their lectures on irony and satire: "Windy," because he's the opposite of long-winded; "Head" because she doesn't use hers; "Sugar" for tough Sally Bowstring, who stabbed Smiley Sorenson with the tip of her rattail comb when he teased her for getting a Twiggy haircut on top of her Mama Cass body.

Now David's friends laugh and shove him around. "So go see the girl, Dutch," they tell him. "Go say hello."

Then David is at my side. "I've seen you at the beach," he says. "You've changed a lot since spring." I smile. He talks. I listen and smile. "Let's walk down by the pit," he suggests.

The pit has been shut down for years. Rain has filled it halfway up.

"Makes an ugly lake, don't you think?" he asks as we stand at its edge.

I say what pops into my mind looking out over the water, washed almost white by the moon: "Stars over snow, and in the west a planet swinging below a star. Look for a lovely thing and you will find it. It is not far. It never will be far."

"Wow. I like that. What is it?"

"Part of a poem. By Sara Teasdale." I look down, embarrassed.

"Miss Teasdale," Dutch grins, "don't tease me with your smooth words." Then, softly, "Do you know more?"

I sit down on the rocky edge of the pit, put my head back, look up at the sleepy sky. I am Sara. I have words. In a dreamy voice I recite: "In the wild soft summer darkness, how many and many a night we two together sat in the park and watched the Hudson, wearing her lights like golden spangles glinting on black satin."

"Miss Hudson," he says after minutes of silence, "may I kiss you goodnight?"

I stand speechless, head down.

David shrugs, then steps away from me. We walk from the edge of the pit toward the party. I tremble on his arm, unkissed.

After David and the other football players leave to make curfew, I stay and look for Barb. One couple thinks she left with a Pelusko kid; another says she's in the woods and still drinking beer. At midnight I know I have to get home. The crowd at the campfire has dwindled to three or four couples and Robert Jensen, who is playing guitar. "There is . . . a house . . . in New Orleans . . ." He knows most of the song by now.

It's hard to ask a Jensen for help, but I do it. "Robert, you know how my dad is. I really need to get home."

"Why didn't Dutch bring you home?"

"Because I didn't ask him to. And Barb . . ."

He raises his eyebrows as if he knows something significant about Barb. "Yeah, I'll get you home." He plays his song through once more.

Robert sips liquor from a small glass bottle. He turns friendly as we wander the path back to the park and his truck. He tells me that his dad's moved down to the Twin Cities and his ma's at the Oasis most nights. I am half listening, half lost in a jumbled surge of emotion. Relief. Remembrance of things David said. Elation . . . and too much beer. I turn sentimental about this wooded trail, the lake, the beach, the school. I walk slowly, sorry to leave this one last, lovely strip of Mesabi land where eagles nest and moss grows thick and damp. The biology teacher's tree identification signs, standing crookedly along the side of the trail, have been posted just for me; like a trail of bread crumbs, they lead me home. "Red maple. Sugar maple. Aspen," I call out. "Birch." At burr oak, I'll be back in Coleraine.

Then Robert helps me gulp five long swigs of straight whiskey and walks me across the park. He tells me how senior year will be. The guys will rush me because I'm looking good; the popular girls will be rude. The new football coach won't let the boys go steady, he says, so Dutch has just broken off with Sue.

Leaves turn colors, fall down, dry up. They rustle like a bride's long taffeta train. Wind follows like a flower girl behind us. I don't remember what happens after that, but in the morning I am alone under the flagpole in Longyear Park. My blue jeans are partway down. Barb rides up in a rusted black Chevrolet driven by the hockey team's goalie. They load me into the backseat. I rock back and forth there, arms hugging my knees. "What have I done?" I ask. "What have I done?"

August ends. Dad begins to click off the TV before the six o'clock news. "Watergate," he says. "Let him drown."

Autumn passes and the first snow blankets the Mesabi Range on Halloween night. I am with David Petrovich, as I often have been this fall. We drive east a few towns to the Calumet pit and watch out the car window as fresh snow soaks red dust from the ground. "Hey, it looks like orange-cherry slush from the Dairy Queen," David tells me. It turns out he likes to play word games, too, as long as we keep it fun.

But there are times when, though words change nothing, a person must tell what is true. "Like a stalk of Indian tobacco, crushed and broken on the ground," I begin. "Like arteries being emptied of their last cool blood. Like a heart drained nearly dry."

"Sshh." Dutch silences me. He kisses me then—a chaste kiss, but I am open to him the way an ore pit is open, or a wound. This time, I do not ask what am I doing, what have I done. I look up beyond the barren rock piles at the starlit night sky from the backseat of David's Buick. I imagine that soft words can make green things grow; can build a dam of sticks and stones to hold back the waves my father says will wash over us all.

"Mickey," David whispers, touching my face with his hand.

Sara. My lips form her name. In my mind I recite part of a poem: "There will be stars over the place forever. There will be stars forever, while we sleep." And in my mind Sara answers back: "Look for a lovely thing and you will find it. It is not far. It never will be far."

1973. Because we don't know what it is to be from Coleraine and to be an American anymore, we protest the school district's dress code by having a sit-in in the front hallway of Greenway High School one week before graduation.

Mr. Greenway watches us from his gold frame on the wall. He is one reason I don't smoke a joint when it is furtively passed; the other reason is my boyfriend. President of our class, David is a throwback to earlier times. He appreciates what this town has done for him and is willing to stand up at booster club meetings and say so. He has scholarships to a college out East from the mining company, the paper mill, and the railroad. There he will make all-Ivy League in football and graduate near the top of his class.

I am the other paper mill scholar in the Class of '73. I plan to attend the community college in Grand Rapids, stay close to home, help out with my younger sisters. "Not ready to leave yet," I tell people when they ask. "Not sure where I want to go. Next year . . . maybe next year."

I leave the sit-in with David when he asks me to. He drives his dad's ore-stained pickup truck down to Longyear Park. We feed pieces of Nut Goodie and then crackers to the ducks at the edge of the lake. David leaves the truck radio on, and we hear my favorite song. It is beautiful, but it is sad: "Sail on silvergirl, sail on by. Your time has come to shine. All your dreams are on their way. See how they shine . . ."

I let David kiss me. Then I give him back his class ring. "You'll meet other girls," I tell him. "You'll want to be free." David does not disagree.

"Like a bridge over troubled water," sing Simon and Garfunkel, "I will lay me down."

On graduation day the state law changes so that eighteen-year-olds can drink. The traditional graduation kegger breaks up early because the local bar is throwing a big party. I go to Dale's Bar. I get drunk.

1983. There's a get-together at the Locker Room on July 2, the weekend before my ten-year class reunion. The walls of this bar are covered with pictures and newspaper clippings from the years when Greenway of Coleraine teams competed in the state hockey tournament. Tonight they're showing a grainy black-and-white film of an overtime loss to St. Paul Johnson.

Sitting with friends and drinking Diet Pepsi, I see my old boy-friend across the crowded room. "Doctor Dutch," I approach him. "Home from the East Coast? What could possibly bring you here?"

"I was hoping I'd run into you," he replies. As if I'm a regular here. As if I'm a part of the softball-bowling-hockey and then out-for-a-beer-afterwards crowd.

"I haven't had a drink in five years," I say.

"I'm glad. I was worried about you." He pats me on the hand the way he might pat a patient in his office.

After that, conversation improves. I confide that I dream about him now and then. In my dreams I just want to talk with him, to convince him I've done all right for myself, like a child seeking her father's approval.

David tells me he dreams of me, too, but that his dreams aren't the least bit paternal. Dressed in a black polo shirt and khaki pants, with bare feet and leather loafers, David might as well be wearing a double-breasted suit in this Iron Range workingman's bar. Six feet, four inches tall, he has tortoise-shell glasses and a few gray hairs at his temples.

I recognize who he reminds me of. "David Petrovich, you'll be the friend of the president someday," I tell him.

"I just might," David agrees.

On July 4 I take my three children to Coleraine for the day. It's the first Fourth of July celebration there in a number of years. Apparently there's been no money for it since the mines began to shut down. We watch the parade: a few floats, the Shriners, the town fire trucks, and the Coleraine City Band. Then I load the kids into our station wagon and drive to the Hillside Cafe in nearby Bovey for an order of home-made french fries and a half-hour out of the sun. As we head toward the café's front door, I have that old Coleraine feeling that someone is watching. I look up and see a video camera filming our approach, taking in the children's rumpled outfits, their sticky faces, their dirty hands and feet.

The young cameraman approaches our booth as we salt french fries and sip Pepsi. He says he's working on a documentation project for the University of Minnesota, filming the decline of the Range. Unemployment, poverty, perseverance. A poet is heading up the project, he says. He is here to tell my story, a story that deserves to be told. "What keeps you here?" he asks, all sad-eyed sincerity. "I really want to know."

I shrug and tell him nothing.

We spend the afternoon in Longyear Park. I do not tell my children that when I was their age, a big carnival with a Ferris wheel and sideshows was always set up here. Today in the park, Shriners in fez caps give burro rides for free. An old hay wagon, hitched to a team of chestnut workhorses, takes the older children up the street and back. I do not tell my children that in the yards of the aging colonials on Lakeview Boulevard Mrs. Mandich and many others served sarma and potica, that in Bovey Mrs. Mazzitelli dished up one hundred plates of spaghetti, that the streets were filled with generations of families long after the fireworks died.

At eight-thirty a crowd begins to gather. I see my mom wheeling

Dad down the boulevard toward the park. "It's Grandpa," calls Hannah, my oldest. She runs toward my parents and climbs up to sit with my dad in his wheelchair. On his lap she finds a small, thin box of sparklers. She climbs down to dance by the lake in the dark, waving the sparkler Grandpa lights for her. And then, because my young ones somehow know what it means to be an American on Independence Day in Coleraine, Minnesota, they stand at attention as the few, shining fireworks boom and explode overhead. They clap their hands, say "oooh" and "ahhh." Hannah turns to my parents and me. "Guys," she sighs, "this is the best place in the world." Her little brother and sister agree.

It is almost midnight by the time I turn onto Roosevelt Avenue and drive toward Grand Rapids, my husband, my home. My children slump deep in their car seats, asleep. I pull over just past the Carnegie library and park in the shadow of the deserted Oliver Mining Company building that sits next to the elementary school overlooking Trout Lake. I fool with the buttons on the car radio, searching for a strong signal—preferably Minnesota Public Radio. But only WKKQ Country comes in this late at night. I let one twangy song play: "From the lakes of Minnesota, to the hills of Tennessee . . . there ain't no doubt I love this place. God bless the USA."

"What the hell," I think, "it's a holiday." I begin to sing along: "If I had to give up all the things I worked for all my life, and start somewhere all over again with just my children and . . ." I click off the radio when the song is over. I listen as my children breathe, as time passes, as fog covers most of Trout Lake. Lee Greenwood is on the radio. President Reagan is in the White House. And I am still in Coleraine, Minnesota, where Mr. John C. Greenway is watching.

Next year, I tell myself. Maybe next year.

NORTH COUNTRY LIVING

Women in the Wood Smoke

Donna Salli

This morning it started to snow. For the first time this season, flakes spiraled across the yard and flew on a brisk diagonal past the picture window. By late afternoon, they'd increased in size and number, and the ground whitened. The towering old pines that give our acreage the look of a cathedral—the pines my ex-woodsman father likes teasingly to put his arms around and say they make him itch to have a crosscut saw—looked, despite their age, a little surprised to be standing there again, ankle deep in it.

Realizing suddenly that the chill I was feeling was not merely a sympathetic shiver for the trees, I leaned down and placed my hand against the baseboard register that runs beneath the window. It was, as I expected, foundation-stone cold.

Pulling my boots on, I reached for the wood pail. As relatively new members of a Greater Minnesota electric cooperative, my husband and I heat our home electrically at a reduced rate. Part of the bargain, however, is that for a given number of hours each season, the cooperative can turn our heat off during peak periods. During those times, we have to heat our house the way folks in these parts did in the old days—scrambling to the woodpile, splitting kindling, tending to the heating of our persons and our property as closely as we would to the needs of a new baby.

We always feel, and express, a certain amount of annoyance on these days. I muttered down the deck steps and across the backyard, feeling put upon and inconvenienced. But as I uncovered the woodpile and began wedging chunks into the misshapen pail—the snow swirling and my mittens collecting wood chips—I began to feel a sneaking satisfaction, an increasingly palpable pleasure as sensations I'd known in childhood quivered and stirred.

As I crumpled paper and stacked the wood in a loose pyre on the grate in the fireplace—then held a match to it—the woman's hands I watched were not *my* hands (hands for the most part unskilled, after years of urban apartment life, in the ways of wood and fire) but those of my mother and of my father's mother, women who built and sustained fires every day, and who worked together to keep me warm and fed.

This all happened around 1959 and 1960, when for a year or so my family lived with my father's parents on their "scrub and rocks" Wisconsin dairy farm. My grandparents had the bedroom downstairs, off the kitchen. The rest of us—Mom, Dad, my two little brothers, and I—shared the upstairs, which, when we first moved in, was one loftlike room with bare two-by-fours. When winter arrived and we started waking up to wreaths of frost around nailheads in the walls beside our beds, my dad insulated the outside walls and divided the space into two rooms, one for him and Mom (and the baby sister who eventually arrived), the other for me and the boys.

Living in that house, we all knew what it meant to be inconvenienced. In many ways, we lived the way the family had during the Depression and World War II—especially the women of the house. Mom and Grandma had cold running water, but no hot; all heating and cooking had to be accomplished on two woodburning stoves; the house didn't even have a toilet or a bath. When so moved, we trekked out to the outhouse by the barn—and at night, when neither parent had the heart or the ambition to carry sleepy kids out to the facilities, the upstairs bedroom rang with the sounds of urine hitting the sides of a galvanized pail. Because we were Finns, we didn't much mind not having a bathtub. We had a sauna—a small, plain shrine of a building built on a hill and surrounded by flowers and raspberry bushes.

Many of my most important lessons about living came from the people in that house, and my first lessons about womanhood—both the pleasure and the difficulty of it—came, intentionally or unintentionally, from my mother and my grandmother. It wasn't always easy for three generations to live in the same house, and that was most apparent to me in the domestic sphere. My grandmother's culinary style was Scandinavian bland, and she was horrified whenever her son's turncoat Finnish wife served an Italian dinner. She stormed around the kitchen on those days calling spices "hay" and mushrooms "worms," muttering in Finnish that people weren't meant to eat things that grew in the dark.

But most of my memories of those two very important women are good ones. I remember Grandma taking my brother and me to the sauna, how amazed I was at her pendulous breasts and her long, dark hair that never had been cut. I picture her in the barn doing the milking, in a ragtag old sweater with a *huivi* wrapped around her head. She kept a can of Crisco high on a shelf for greasing the cows' teats, and the highlight of milking for me was dipping my fingers into the creamy smoothness of it. Even now, my nostrils dilate at the thought of the vinegar she soaked my foot in once, when I stepped on a nail. But most of all I remember her late at night, sitting on the edge of her bed playing her *kantele* and singing in Finnish. The combination of her voice and the zitherlike instrument lent an eerie note to those nights that I can hear still.

My memories of my mother at that time are more house-centered. I see her heating water on the woodstove and wrestling it to the old wringer washer in the basement, or bathing my toddler brother in a little red tub on the kitchen floor. I feel her sitting between my other brother and me, reading a bedtime story or poem to us in the bed we shared. In that house with wondrously few amenities, our mother managed to inspire a deep regard for beauty and the written word. But most of all, I remember the cold winter mornings of first grade, when she would go down long before me to fix my breakfast and warm my clothes, how she later knelt and dressed me in front of the open oven door.

What I took away from that place were the values I was given there, values that are still very much the foundation stones of my adult life: to live as simply as a person can these days, making the most out of the least; to look for beauty in humble and unlikely persons and things; and, most important, never to place the needs of the body before those of the spirit and mind.

I shouldn't complain that now and then I have to tend a fire. To this day, when I hear snapping embers, when I smell wood smoke, I'm in front of that old stove again—a little girl in white tights and white slip, trying to twirl on her toes and no doubt impossible to dress. For a moment, my mother is younger than I am now. My grandmother is alive and stirring in the next room. Half of me is shivering—the other, warm.

Sugar Bush

Anne M. Dunn

I remember the crusty snow crunching under our boots as we broke trail into the sugar bush. I remember that the cooking scaffold looked like a lonely skeleton with its arms flung out in welcome.

Like a grid, the scaffold shadow marked the place where we would build the fire. Digging down through the snow and matted leaves, we prepared a fireplace on the rich, dark forest soil. The children had already gathered bundles of dry sticks, which they wigwammed over bits of paper and birch bark. The wigwam was lit on the wind-blown side and fed with larger sticks until a brisk blaze was leaping toward the sky.

Because we had no buildings there, at the end of the past sugaring season we had stacked our inverted catch-cans and cooking pails near the scaffold and covered them with tar paper held in place with heavy poles. Each year when we arrived, we dug them out, filled the pails with fresh snow, and hung them from the scaffold with strong wires. Tile fire licked eagerly at the black pails as we added more snow, until we had enough hot water to wash and rinse three hundred catch-cans.

I have an especially vivid memory of the felling of a large dead maple. To our dismay we discovered it had been home to several flying squirrels. We quickly counted them as they glided down among the trees to seek new hiding places. It's quite unusual to see them during the day, and seven is more than most people will see in a lifetime.

As the men cut and split the wood, the women and children hauled it to camp on a long toboggan. There, they log-cabin stacked it like a fortress wall around the scaffold. The wall of wood would serve as a windbreak near the fire, where the kegs would dry quickly if it should rain or snow. It took several days to get the wood ready. We knew there would be little time for gathering wood when the sap began to run.

When we had stacked enough wood . . . we went home to wait.

I watched the box elders near our home because we know that when the box elders begin to weep, it's time to tap the maples.

In late winter, the sap rises up into the trees to begin another season of growth. The process is triggered by the fluctuating temperatures of cold, freezing nights followed by warm, thawing days.

How anxious we became as the days passed. At last we saw bright tears glistening in the branches of the box elders. The sap was running!

We returned to camp with a brace and bit and a box of clean taps. The children distributed catch-cans. Small trees were tapped once on the sunrise side, so they would begin to flow early in the day. Larger trees would produce more sap and could be tapped more than once. One great tree held five cans well-spaced around its huge trunk. We called the tree "Grandfather."

We stood together to witness the tapping of the first tree. As the bit was turned, a long curl of moist wood was drawn out. When the bit was removed, a spout was placed in the hole and a can was quickly hung in place. We watched a drop of sap appear, glitter in the sunlight, fall from the spout, and splash into the bottom of the can with a musical *ting*. With that drop . . . another harvest had begun!

Because the sweet-tasting sap is only about 3 percent sugar, it may take more than thirty gallons of sap to produce one gallon of syrup. Boiling the sap to make syrup is long, hard work.

But although the sugar bush is a place of intense work, it is also a place of spiritual renewal and personal enrichment. It's hard to imagine a better place to be in March.

If I got to camp early, I'd find the sap still frozen in the spouts. I'd lay wood for a large fire, about eight feet long and three feet wide, fill the cooking pails with sap from the storage barrels, and hang the pails over the fire. Then I'd brew a pot of sap coffee.

As the sun climbed into the sky, the grove began to warm and I'd walk away from the snapping fire to listen to the sap song. I'd hear it begin far away. *Ting*. The sap was thawed. *Ting*. It fell into waiting catch-cans. *Ting. Ting*. Soon I was surrounded by the happy rhythm. But as the cans began to fill, the song subsided . . . for only empty cans sing.

When I was young I used to think, "If we did not come to release the maple sap, life would not return to the land. For life flows from this grove into all the world." Now, I think it strange to imagine we might deny spring by refusing to tap the maples. But nevertheless, I find it difficult to laugh at the wisdom of such foolishness.

Although the sugar bush enriched my life with quiet memories, it would never be complete without the laughter of happy children.

The children spent many hours swinging in the arms of an ancient maple broken by storms and years. The giant seemed unwilling to resign itself to the earth and, propped up on huge limbs, it invited the children to many adventures. They called it the love tree, because they loved to play there.

The children also learned to be comfortable with wild things. Near the camp, two osprey made their summer home. Their ragged-looking nest clung to the top of a dead poplar. How eagerly we welcomed their return from the south, as they circled our camp like great winged sentinels!

The quiet of the warming days was often broken by the staccato of hungry woodpeckers. Squirrels and later chipmunks visited us for handouts and flicked their tails, saluting our generosity.

One year, two playful weasels came to live in our wood stack and made us laugh with their favorite game. They'd chase each other through the stack and suddenly pop up between the wood sticks. Then, almost before we saw them leave, they were blinking at us from somewhere else. They went so fast that it was like watching six weasels running around in the woodpile.

In the evenings we sat together in the glow of the fire, lost in private worlds of thought. But as the darkness gathered, it seemed to draw us nearer to each other. Families were knit and friendships sealed around the campfire.

Each night, we carried our precious burden of steaming syrup home. Walking down the trail, I felt close to the people who had come to the grove long ago. I could almost see them walking among the trees, peering into catch-cans and nodding in satisfaction. I could almost hear the mud sucking softly at their feet, as they went to warm themselves at our abandoned fire still glowing with bright coals.

The closing of the sugar bush was celebrated with a thanksgiving feast. Then, one by one, we picked up our packs to leave. Single file, we moved down the muddy trail. One by one, we paused at the turn in the path to look back.

The quiet woods, the crisp spring air, the cry of the owl, and the echo of tradition had had their way with us. To ourselves, we promised to return again . . . when the box elders begin to weep.

The Tree

Jeanne Grauman

Christmas Eve day was always packed with things to do on our northern Minnesota farm. Even ordinary chores seemed special somehow. We cleaned till things shone like my grandpa's bald head. We swept, mopped the floors, and dusted all the shelves. The dining room always got the most attention. All the furniture was moved around to make room for the Christmas tree. My Dad or my brother Brad usually got the tree from the back forty. Getting the Christmas tree seemed to be the best job of all. Everyone ooohed, ahhhed, and said what a fine specimen it was. It always turned out to be the best tree ever, no matter what it looked like. Christmas never really started until the tree was pulled through the door. The getters came home like conquering kings.

Dad was one of those people who was bigger than life. The kind who could fill up a room just by walking in. He was from the old school and had an air of authority about him that fit like a second skin. He was never one to say much. He didn't have to. You just naturally did whatever you could to please him. Even other grown-ups did. I don't know how to explain why we wanted to please him. Maybe it was because he always expected more from himself than he did from anyone else. If he put his trust in you, you knew you'd earned something worthwhile. It made you feel bigger somehow even if you hadn't grown an inch.

I remember the year I asked Dad to let me get the tree. He said I could. Only I'd have to use a saw instead of an ax, since I was only seven. I felt myself swell with importance. Maybe I wasn't artistic like Kathy or beautiful like Margie, sweet like Cindy, or even small like Michelle. Maybe I was too young to use the ax. Still, if Dad trusted me to get the tree, I must be something special. Everything seemed wonderful. Me, Jeanne, I would be the one coming through the door heralding the start of Christmas. Everyone would scooch close to the walls to make room when I pulled the pine smelling glad tidings through the door. They'd all oooh and ahhh and would know that I was something special.

It wasn't until I actually got started that some of the wonder wore off. You see, if I was going to get that tree, I'd have to go to the back forty. I was scared to go out to Wolf Hill alone. That's what we called the back forty because every night the wolves would howl from there. They would come out of that Itasca County swamp, up onto the hill, and cry to each other for half the night. I always heard them real good, because my bedroom was on the back of the house. I would scare the daylights out of my little sisters and brothers with stories about Wolf Hill. The only trouble with that was now I was going out there by myself—alone. Those stories sort of came back and scared me too. The more I thought about those eerie cries, the less I wanted to go out there.

I considered the importance of my mission. The pride, the praise, to say nothing of the trust Dad put in me. With this in mind, I squished my fears as far down as I could. I was going to get that Christmas tree.

I dressed up good and warm and headed for the toolshed. The cold air felt good on my cheeks, but it burned the inside of my nose when I breathed real deep. It was dark inside the shed, even with the light on, because there weren't any windows. All the walls had big brown spikes in them where Dad hung up the outdoor tools. The shovels, rakes, and hoes hung in neat rows on one side. Pitchforks, pry bars, a washtub, and lots more interesting stuff on the other. The saws and axes were on the very back wall. It was the shortest one, yet it still held a lot of saws.

There was a huge one that hung from the ceiling to the floor. It had wood handles on either end, with teeth the size of a lion's. I'd used that saw before. Brad and I took over getting the firewood after my older brothers, Billy and Murray, joined the navy. We used that two-man saw to get it. I also learned that when you cut a tree you never push the saw, only pull, or it pinches and stops dead in its tracks. Not only did it hurt your arm, it made my brother mad as heck. There were little bitty saws, about the size of a table knife, and a whole bunch of in-between ones. Until this moment, I hadn't realized how many saws there were. I looked them over and lifted a few of them off the spikes. Finally, I settled on one I could swing around pretty well. I thought, "If one of those wolves comes around, I'll use this saw like a sword and I'll slice his head off." Now that I'd picked my weapon, it was time to look for the tree.

Well, I started for the woods. But right there at the edge of the backyard was the most perfect tree I'd ever seen. I wouldn't have to go to Wolf Hill after all. I could cut this tree without ever losing sight of the house.

My dad must have seen me through the window. I'd just cleared enough snow to lie down and sawed back and forth about twice when the sound of his boots crunching in the snow stopped me. I peered out from under the tree through the branches. He just stood there for a while looking at me. Finally he asked, "What are you doing?" I figured he probably already knew, so I didn't say anything. Then he asked, "Do you remember my planting that tree a few years back?"

When he said that, a picture did come to my mind of him sweating as he dug holes and carried umpteen buckets of water. I still didn't say anything. Instead, I crawled out from under my perfect Christmas tree dragging the saw with me. He looked at me again and shook his head like he couldn't believe what he was seeing. His eyes were fixed on the object in my hand. There was another one of those eternal pauses. And a long sigh that made puffs in the cold air like smoke. Then in one of those deep, tight kind of voices he said, "I think you should put my meat saw back in the shed. I'll probably need it sharp come butchering time."

I saw his boots face the other direction heading back from where they came. I didn't see anything else, because from the time his eyes focused on the saw, I couldn't seem to lift my head. I hadn't said a word the whole time. At first I didn't know what to say, but later my throat felt so big it wouldn't let anything through—not even "I'm sorry," or to tell him about the wolves.

All my dreams of glory disappeared like the smoke from his breath. I was a disappointment, a failure. My feet felt like they were frozen to the ground. I could hear muffled laughter and the clanking of pans coming from the kitchen, but home seemed a million miles away. I felt homesick and lost right there in my own backyard. I could feel my tears turn to ice as they ran down my face. The cold didn't feel good anymore, just cold. The fuzz on my mittens froze in little spikes where I'd wiped my nose. It was all I could do to catch a little air in the great hiccuping breaths I was taking. It took a long time to put the saw away. I stood around by the shed, wanting to go home but not quite knowing how to find my way back in.

The slam of the storm door warned me someone was coming outside. At first I scrunched my face against the tar paper wall of the shed, but my face stuck to it. So I put my mittens over my face and leaned against it that way. My back was to the house, so maybe no one would see me. I didn't want anyone to see me or talk to me. The footsteps kept coming right toward me, but I didn't take my face away from the shed to see who it was. My brother

Brad's voice said, "Hey, Jeanne, Dad thought maybe you'd like to come with me and get the tree." The steps went right on by and I heard the shed door squeak open as he went in to get the ax. The tight belt around my chest started to loosen and it got easier to breathe. By the time the shed door opened again and the hasp clinked shut, it seemed Christmas and home weren't so far away after all. Dad must think I'm okay if he sent me along to help.

I followed my brother through the deep, heavy snow. We went across the field, over Wolf Hill, to the edge of the swamp. He had long legs but he walked slowly, dragging his feet so I could keep up. He said, "We're going to get the biggest tree ever because there's two of us to carry it." He didn't seem a bit frightened going over Wolf Hill and into the swamp. You know what? Neither was I. We found the biggest and best tree on the place in no time at all. My job was really important because I had to carry the top end of the tree. If I carried it too close to the end, it would break off, so I had to be real careful. Even though the trail was broken, it was a lot of work coming home. I fell down a couple times—but I never broke the top off! I could just imagine the look on their faces when they saw the size of this tree.

I didn't get to see everybody's face when we brought the tree in because I was on the end that comes in last. But I knew just what they'd look like. Mom would be there first to open the door. She would suck in a great gulp of air like she was surprised and her eyes would be overflowing with love and pride. Everyone else would be scooched up against the walls to make room for the tree to come through. Then I was inside and the warm air hit me! The smell of fresh cinnamon rolls and bread seemed to be fighting with the tangy odor of baking ham. But the best smell of all was the scent of pine.

That night, coming home from midnight service, I rode in the very back of the station wagon with Cindy and Michelle. Mom, Dad, Ronnie, and Stephen, the baby, sat in front. Brad, Kathy, and Margie sat in the middle seat. I didn't mind sitting way in the back because you always got a window that way. I pressed my face on the cold glass so I could watch the moon make diamonds on the snowy fields. As we turned down the driveway, the lights from the farm reached out like welcoming arms. Prince barked a hello and we all piled into the house.

No one bothered to put their shoes in neat rows. Even Mom left hers in the middle of the entryway. Someone was still humming a Christmas hymn we sang in church. We gathered around the table to hear Dad read the Christmas story and eat our holiday feast. The talk around the table was as varied as the dishes being passed. When the dinner came to a close, everyone sat back—content and full. Dad looked over his shoulder at the tree and said, "Even if it wasn't your first choice, and it wasn't cut with my meat saw, I still think it's the best one yet." Except his voice wasn't tight. It was open and warm and his eyes crinkled up at the edges from his smile. Everyone was laughing at my mistake. I felt my face grow hot, like when you hang your head over the toaster to make sure your bread's not burning, but I laughed too. Then a thought struck me that made me laugh even harder. Dad thought I'd made a mistake by picking the meat saw. Only he didn't know about the wolves. If I had met one of those hairy beasts, that meat saw would have been the perfect weapon to have along.

Ice Harvest

Justine Kerfoot

When we carried a bucket of chipped ice to a cabin for evening cocktails, or packed fish in boxes mixed with sawdust and ice, our guests gave little thought to its origin. Our ice did not come in formed blocks from ice machines. We cut it from the lake in midwinter and stored it in our icehouse. The ice we put up in winter was the lodge's only refrigeration for the entire summer.

The icehouse was close to the lake because we had to haul twenty-five to thirty tons of ice into it every winter. Icehouses varied in size from eight feet by ten feet to fourteen feet by fourteen feet, with double walls six to eight feet high, insulated with sawdust. There were two openings in the building. The front opening was of full door size, and boards were placed across it as the icehouse was filled. On the opposite wall was a large window-size opening where we shoveled in the sawdust.

When we first built our icehouse, a logging camp was located nearby. Truckloads of sawdust from the camp were hauled in and piled cone-shape next to the new building. We used the same sawdust year after year; seldom did it need replenishing. In other remote locations where sawdust was not available, sphagnum moss was used effectively as an insulator, but it deteriorated and had to be replaced each year.

For us the ice harvest started directly after New Year's. Our lake froze over in mid-December; the smaller lakes froze a couple of weeks sooner. We allowed ten days for the ice to become safe; then we measured out the ice field. We located the field far enough out so the saw wouldn't hit bottom and in an area where the ice had frozen smooth. Now we would have to shovel the ice field after each new snow. A layer of snow insulated the ice and prevented it from freezing deeper. If the snow became heavy enough, it could flood the ice, creating a layer of slush ice, which does not have a lasting quality like clear blue ice. When we harvested the ice, we had to trim off and discard slush ice.

The ideal time for ice harvest was when we could estimate the ice's thickness at nineteen to twenty inches. Often around that time Nature delighted in sweeping through with a bitter wind and temperatures of twenty below zero. Then we were in a bind: If we waited for warmer weather, the ice was thicker, heavier, and much harder to handle. If the days turned even colder, the saw froze in the cut even as it was pulled up and down. Once we started the harvest, we had to continue until the icehouse was filled.

As the Indians on the far shore noticed our first stirrings on the ice, they would start snowshoeing across the lake to help us. They gave us a hand each day, as a friendly gesture, until the job was done.

It usually took two or three days to harvest ice: saw the cakes, pull them into the icehouse, break open the frozen sawdust pile, and shovel the sawdust into the house, packing it around the edges of each layer. The ice harvest was work, but it was also a neighborly event in which we were all involved. And when we finished we had a feeling of accomplishment. As Alice Brandt of Poplar Lake said to me years later, "We had fun putting up ice, didn't we?" It was an annual challenge that we all accepted and dealt with.

The tools we used to put up ice were an axe, a spud bar, an ice chisel, an ice saw, and two very large ice tongs. First we scratched a grid on the bare ice for guidelines to saw the cakes straight and of a manageable size. Next we chiseled a hole through the ice, large enough to insert the saw. A channel was then cut along one side of the field and broken out with a spud bar. The cakes were sawed along the guidelines and broken out. Then we used the tongs to drag the ice cakes out of the water, to the icehouse, and then up a wooden ramp leading to the inside of the building.

I always had a terrible urge to figure out a way to do a job without "bulling it." My successes were about fifty-fifty. Bill shuddered when one of my inspirations was about to develop. He figured the job could be accomplished the regular way in less time than it took me to get all my rigging in place.

One time after shoveling the snow to make a road to the icehouse, I attached one end of a long rope to the car and extended the rope via a set of pulleys through the icehouse and out to the field where it was attached to the tongs. On signal I drove off with such speed that the ice skidded up the chute into the icehouse and hit the outer wall with a thud. This system would have worked, but we were too far apart to receive signals fast enough to keep us from knocking the building apart with the cakes of ice. With reluctance I dismantled my contrivance and tried a new approach.

I hitched the dogs to my long toboggan and took them to the ice field. After we pulled the cakes from the water we slid them onto the toboggan. On command the dogs would pull the load of cakes to the chute. John, our lead dog, shortly learned to turn the team around as soon as the cakes were unloaded, take the team back to the ice hole, turn the team again, and wait to be loaded for the return. I came out ahead with this system as long as the dogs cooperated.

Toward the end of the day the dogs would tire. As they turned to pass one another, one dog would be jostled, which would start a few complaining woofs and end in a glorious dogfight with dogs, harnesses, and ropes all a tangled, snarling, nipping mess.

It is difficult to untangle such a melee of uncooperative beasts. I tried throwing pepper in their faces so they would have to sneeze and couldn't bite, but usually the wind wafted the spice toward me. Finally I just waded in and pulled them apart, whereupon they lopped against each other completely exhausted.

Walter Plummer and Abie Cook took turns with Bill on the sawing, and Butchie helped me push the cakes up and place them in layers in the icehouse. If I could place the ice cakes in the same arrangement as they were in the lake, everything would fit together snugly like an interlocked jigsaw puzzle. I had been trying to teach Butchie to read and write and to expand her use of English. Suddenly it dawned on me we were back to essentials that needed no expansion: "You pull; I push."

Putting up ice was hard and heavy work. The higher we stacked the ice in the icehouse the more confining the space. As we neared the top it became increasingly difficult to shovel sawdust into the foot-wide space between the ice and the walls.

Our ice harvest was a round-robin effort of neighbors. Often John Clark, our trapper friend across the lake, would come over to help us. In turn we would help him put up his ice. After these jobs were completed, Bill and I, along with one or two of our Indian neighbors, would go down the lake to fill Charlie Olson's small icehouse.

Finding Symmetry in a Rock Pile

Robert Treuer

It has become increasingly important to me to strive for certain balances in my life, bringing symmetry to everyday living. Much of my work takes place indoors, all the more impelling me out of doors on walks, skis, snowshoes, by canoe. In order to suit me, these activities fit into the woof and warp of the day. Preferably, I would be able to step outside and do what I wish, as work and obligations allow.

It is the same with physical labor; working with wood, stone, and earth is counterweight to my intellectual pursuits, to the efforts in writing, in music, and in other fields. The contrast makes me appreciate the tactile and sensual rewards of physical work, even of drudgery. I relish the smell of cedar, pine, oak, and other woods in my carpentry pursuits, though the olfactory bouquet is no *succor* when I hit my finger with the hammer. Whether planting trees or spading the garden (which I do without significant enthusiasm, and amid much complaining), I am aware of the feel of the earth, of the variety of smells of the soil—dry, moist, lean, rich. It goes without saying that I am equally aware of the fertile manure pile that my wife had so thoughtfully delivered and dumped downwind from our bedroom window.

There is a particular fascination, bordering on a love affair, in working with stone. There have been occasions to help a neighbor clear rocks from a field, piling a cairn in a far corner; to build a stone wall; to split rock for fancy work; to construct a retaining wall to retard erosion in a cut. Now the time is here to riprap stone at each end of a culvert and along a steep bank bordering the driveway, at the place where it winds up the hill.

A neighboring farmer is happy to have his rock pile hauled out of the corner of a field and donate it to my needs.

"I know every one of those rocks personally," his wife tells me. "Picked most of them by hand, and a few we had to put chains around and pull with the tractor. Couple we had to use two tractors. Just be sure you don't let the cattle out when you open the gate. If they get in the green alfalfa this time of year they'll get sick and die."

I promise to be careful, to drive only along the fence line and not across the field, and to shut the gate entering and leaving.

I am lucky and get Andy Talevson to bring his big bulldozer with backhoe and his dump trucks, the condition being that I would work with him. The dump trucks look like museum pieces but the motors purr.

Andy is gray haired, pink cheeked, a stocky, short bull of a man with the smile of a pixie; it starts with a twinkle and then unfolds slowly, but it is unstoppable once it begins, his personality warming everyone around. He is much more than a person involved in machinery and equipment, in grease and repairs and loud noises; like every human being, he has many facets to his self, a man of sensibilities and caring with an eye for beauty, a heavy equipment operator who is environmentalist, gardener, college student, parent. A man who would sooner lose time and squeak a huge machine between two trees than roar through and knock them over.

"First thing in the morning," says Andy, "you'll be ready."

It is a question, but said as a flat statement accompanied by arching eyebrows.

"I'll be ready." It is a safe commitment for me to make. When Andy says he'll start early in the morning it is about lunchtime for the rest of the world, but he will expect to work until it is pitch dark or later. It is just that his concept of the workday is a bit off the norm. But he is the best, and I cherish him besides.

In midafternoon the loaded trucks arrive. I had begun to fret by then, expecting a phone call to the neighboring farm to help Andy, his son, and his helpers. But they apparently concluded I would be more hindrance than help, and they surprise me with the first installment of boulders. Andy untwines himself from the cab of the bigger truck and inspects the terrain, Napoleon at Austerlitz preparing for the battle.

"There's some peat down there," he announces. "We could put a few really big ones there, spot them around, for a rock garden. Flowers." This has nothing to do with riprapping the culvert, where receding spring ice and runoff pose a problem, or with the erosion along the driveway. Andy just takes it for granted he will take care of these, and he has his eye on the aesthetics of the job.

"Bring me some big ones," he instructs his helpers. "From the north end of the rock pile." He climbs on the bulldozer, parked there the day before, and starts the machine. Piles, mounds of stone are pushed to the culvert ends and rolled down. How will I ever get some of the bigger ones, weighing several hundred pounds, in position? I am reluctant to ask Andy to help with individual stones; he is already doing more than I had expected.

"When the backhoe is attached I'll spot the bigger ones," he calls down from the roaring machine. "Don't bother with them now. Just figure out where you want them. There's a pretty one, I'll just roll it aside for the rock garden." He is off, pursuing his vision of a Japanese contemplation stone weighing nearly half a ton that he seems to think will be beautiful amid the ferns. It is a whitish granite, almost limestone in color, a prehistoric egg among craggy and odd-shaped greens, pinks, and ochres.

I pause from my end of the job, placing stones in a slanting wall from the creek up toward the driveway, anchoring stone upon stone, shoveling sand to lay each one, stepping the next stone up. They feel rough, but a pattern, a system evolves in how they should go together. Andy has infected me with the vision, the sense of how it might, how it should be.

"Could we take four big ones out to the end of the driveway," I ask, "where the kids wait for the school bus? They'd each have a sitting rock."

"We'll pick some smooth ones," he answers, casting his eye around. The trucks keep hauling, and he tells the drivers he wants more "big ones."

"And next time dump them farther up the drive," he instructs. "I'll spot for you when you come back." He has very definite ideas.

Several loads later he has found the perfect sitting stones, and he picks them out with delicate movements, handling the controls of the rumbling and roaring monster he drives with the delicacy of a watchmaker.

One boulder too large for me to move catches my eye. It is blue? Green? When the rain has washed it the true color will be discernible. There are deep, parallel ridges grooved in it, about an inch deep, nearly two inches wide. It is a piece of granite bedrock that had been beneath a glacier, and through the inexorable, slow movement of the glacial mass tens of thousands of years ago, smaller stones caught in the glacier bottom had gouged, grooved the pattern.

I manage to tip the mass over and find similar grooves on the sides of the rock as well.

"Hey, Andy," I call. "Here's one with deep glacial rill."

He stops the machine, dismounts to look, and we contemplate

this ancient piece of original life and earth—this mother of us all, welded of tiny pieces and bits of rock and matter by volcanic lava, by the action of some Mount St. Helens billions of years ago in some Precambrian eruption; then cooled, buried, upheaved, grilled, ultimately broken, working its way up in a farmer's field over the hundreds of millions of years. It is a reminder of the incredible forces and the time that has elapsed in the life flow and processes that produced us.

We go back to our work, then the machine is throttled down again.

"Where do you want that one?" Andy asks. I had not said anything but he knew I would want it for my own, in some private place among huge pines, a centerpiece in the cathedral of trees to look at, to contemplate, at times sit upon.

I look up at the hill, and he nods. "I think I can get it there without disturbing anything."

Sugar Camp

Susan Carol Hauser

Rolland grew up in the log cabin that is our living room. In the 1920s and 1930s, a "tote road," a wagon trail between towns, cut across the south field and along the east edge of the homestead's forty acres. Between the tote road and the house stood the grove of trees that is now our sugar bush.

Rolland and his father did not sugar there. Twenty trees were not worth the effort. Instead they hitched up the horses to the sleigh and went to their sugar camp: west from the house, down the hill to the meadow that is now a swamp, across the meadow and the ford in the creek, up the slope on the other side, past grandma's house, and out onto the peninsula that separates our bay of Mud Lake from the lake itself.

The road down the peninsula was wide enough for the sleigh, but there was also room in the woods to drive the team among the trees themselves. The shrubby undergrowth that keeps humans at arm's length today requires warmth and good sun. The old forests were cool and dark, the crowns of the mature trees holding hands in summer to keep the sun at bay.

In March, in the daylight, Rolland and his father took the sleigh and team and went to the sugar bush on the point. Using a breast drill, they tapped the trunks of two hundred maples. Into each hole they tapped a spile, a curl of metal, fashioned at home. On each spile they hung a metal pail with a little tin roof to keep out snow, rain, leaves, and the dust of the forest.

Every morning and evening, Rolland and his dad made the rounds of the sugar bush to pick sap, guiding the team and sleigh along the snow path between the trees. They emptied the collection pails into five-gallon milk cans and took the whole lot back to the "arch," the place where they boiled off. At the end of the morning pick, Rolland returned home to sleep. At the end of the evening pick, Rolland's father returned home.

Rolland stayed at the sugar camp all night, boiling one to two hundred gallons of sap, as his father had done during the day. One at a time, as the level lowered, he lifted the five-gallon cans and added sap to the four foot by two foot by ten inches deep metal evaporating pan that they'd had made in town. He teased at the fire to keep it hot but not too hot, and sometimes he laid back on the ground and listened to the conversation of the nighttime forest.

When the day's sap run was boiled down to about a half inch in the pan, Rolland poured it off, back into the five-gallon milk cans. In the morning, his father came with the team and the sleigh, and they made the rounds of the taps and took the sap to the arch, and Rolland took the cans with the near-syrup and went across the creek, and across the meadow, and up the hill to the log cabin.

His mother finished the syrup at the kitchen stove. She poured it into kitchen pans, and kept the fire hot but not too hot, and when the syrup drew two beads from a metal spoon, she poured it off into jugs and corked it. When they went to town, they took along a few jugs of maple syrup to trade and to sell.

When Rolland married he no longer sugared on the point, but he and Jenny helped sugar at a neighbor's. For as far as one could walk in the forest, it seemed, pails hung from trees. Families gathered. The grownups hung out around the fire, talking. The children ran into the trees and back, never getting too far away. The young adults volunteered to pick at the farthest trees, the ones out of sight where, the stories say, there was kissing. At the end of the day, the near-syrup was taken into the house and the women finished it at the stove.

As I stand at the kitchen sink wetting the filters I use to strain the sap, I look down the field and to the right where a small rise in the land creates a north slope. Yes, there is still snow there. The end of it. Even the cat ice is gone now from the wet spots in the sugar bush. This afternoon when I picked sap, the leaves, the last of their moisture given off to the spring sun, crackled underfoot and under the wheels of my cart.

I squeeze the excess water out of the four sheets of felt, layer them in the colander, and set the colander in the heavy aluminum pot that was my mother's pressure cooker. The lid long ago went its own way, but this pot is perfect for finishing syrup. It is heavy, so the syrup will not burn easily, and the sides are high, so it cannot easily boil over, though it can and does.

I retrieve the small, shallow aluminum bowl and the shallow dipper from the dishwasher, pick up one leather glove from the stand by the door, and take my apparatus out to the kettle. Bill has pulled the skirt away and is spreading out the last of the fire. In the bottom of the kettle bubbles break on the less than a gallon of near-syrup that remains from the ten gallons simmered for six hours.

I sit in one of the lawn chairs with the pot and colander on my lap and watch as Bill dips the long-handled ladle into the sap and pours it back out into the kettle. It is dark amber, partly because it is laced with "sugar sand," a natural sediment in maple syrup, partly because it is getting late in the season, and partly because we boil in a trade kettle and each batch leaves behind a candied film that cooks into subsequent batches.

One holding pail of today's pick is set between me and the fire in case the sap in the kettle decides to foam up and turn to hard candy. A few tablespoons will settle it back down. The rest of the day's pick is in holding pails sitting in and beside the cart. We'll cook it tomorrow.

Around me the day quiets and prepares to shut down. The chickadees and flickers have quit their banter. The breeze has slowed, leaving silent last year's tall, dried goldenrod that fills up the empty spaces in the grove. Halfway between due west and due north, the sun closes in on the horizon.

The embers that Bill dispersed from under the kettle have given up their glow, and the coming on of the evening air has relieved the kettle of some of its heat. I move to Bill's side and hold the house pot while he reaches down with the aluminum bowl, dips out sap, and pours it into the colander. The hot bubbles settle out as the sap meets the cool, wet felt, and slowly the syrup-to-be seeps through into the pot, leaving sugar sand and kettle debris in the filters.

When only spoonfuls are left in the kettle, Bill switches to the dipper and rescues every bit that he can, then picks up the nearby sap pail and pours a few gallons into the kettle to keep the left-overs from burning.

Balancing the pot on the rim of the kettle, I retrieve the leather glove from my pocket and use it as a hot pad so I can hold the now heavy pot in both hands, one on the perpendicular handle, one underneath, with the glove to protect my skin from the heat. Bill takes a last poke at the ashes, and we turn together and walk to the house.

Inside the door, I set the pot on the stand, take off my jacket, and hang it on the rack next to the parka I wore the first few weeks. The aura of smoke and sugar surrounds both garments, and in few minutes, when I get the sap cooking, the perfume of maple will permeate the house.

In the kitchen, I set the pot by the sink and hold the colander up so the sap can finish draining. Then I put the colander in the sink and move the pot to the stove.

Now begin the last two hours of the day's work. Unlike the outside tasks, which can be done at leisure, this cooking takes attention and precision. I hook a candy thermometer onto the pot, turn the burner on to medium heat, and watch as bubbles seek the surface and break into air.

In a few minutes the sap is back up to a simmer, about two hundred and twenty degrees. I turn the burner down a bit, and begin the syrup-dinner dance. Get something out of the fridge, check the syrup. Start the peas cooking, check the syrup. Cross the room to set the table. Listen to the syrup.

Even in the house finishing pot, syrup sings when it is about to boil up. A slight hiss. A warning. A promise. If I hear it, and I am quick enough, I can get to the pot before it goes over, before the huge golden bubbles leap the pan and spread themselves over the stove top and down into the burner.

If I am not quick enough, I have a mess to clean up, and syrup to rescue. I take the pot to the sink, wipe off the sides and bottom, return it to a clean burner, and turn the heat on low. When the first burner is cool, I remove it and then remove the cup I'd set under it to catch overflow. Then I take a spatula and scrape up every grain of syrup that has solidified on the stove top and put it in a bowl. We'll munch on it. I scrape the spatula clean, then lick it cleaner. If no one is looking, I lean down to the stove and lick up the last tracings with my tongue.

It happens at least once a season. Sometimes early, when I am not yet attuned to the rhythms of sugaring. Sometimes later, when I am made careless by luck. Today, as the sugar content increases in the sap in the pot, so do I reduce the heat of the burner.

When dinner is ready, I turn the burner way down so I can eat, but even then get up occasionally to inspect the dark, glossy surface. After dinner, I turn up the heat again, and also heat a teakettle full of water. While it comes to a boil I set four pint jars and a half-pint jar in the sink. Then I put five canning lids and rings, a funnel, and a pair of tongs into a bowl in the sink. When the water is ready, I pour it into the jars and the bowl, and I am ready for the syrup.

When I first brought the sap into the house it was still thin relative to syrup. It easily slipped off a metal spoon and back into the pot. As it reduced, it began to hold on the spoon, but still flowed off in a single stream. Now, as it gets closer to syrup, it hangs onto the spoon and struggles to pull together into a single bead, which reluctantly drops off into the pot. Soon it will not be able to manage that, will separate and simultaneously draw two long threads on its way back to the pan.

By that time I have taken out the candy thermometer, because the level in the one-gallon pot has reduced from a few inches from the top to a few inches from the bottom, and the thermometer is no longer accurate. But the spoon is, and when the sap consistently draws two beads, I transfer the jars and lids to a clean cloth on the counter next to the stove and finish today's maple syrup.

I lift the pot by its outstretched handle and, using the funnel, fill three of the pints to a half-inch from their tops. Then, depending on how much is left, I fill another pint or the half-pint. Moving quickly, I set a lid on each one, then take a wet cloth in each hand and screw the lids down, and then give them one more turn twice, and once again to be sure, and then tip them for a moment on their sides to further sterilize the lids, and then set them in a row on the counter, and then stand back and contemplate.

Three and one-half pints. A decent day's take from twenty maples. It is seven in the evening. Bill started the outside fire at eleven in the morning. I step into the living room and announce the outcome to Bill, and we talk about the ten gallons of sap sitting outside in the dusk, waiting for tomorrow's boiling, and we wonder if it will freeze tonight, and the sap will run again tomorrow, or if it will stay as warm as it is now, forty-five degrees.

And I sit for a minute before I return to wash up the sugaring dishes and rinse out the filters. The sun is at my favorite sunset trajectory. It casts a beam through the entryway window onto the side of the mahogany piano, onto the small table stacked with books, across the top of the television, casting on the far wall shadows of the trinkets we keep there, a brass elephant, a marble donkey, a glass goat, and lands last on the bookcase in the corner where it ignites a row of pictures of children, parents, siblings, and friends.

Twice each year this blade of light cuts through the armor of the house, forecasting spring or fall. It saddens me as much as it brings pleasure. Even in the timeless time of sugaring, time is passing.

Ping. A syrup jar in the kitchen seals itself, the metal lid announcing that it is has yielded to the heat of the syrup and is sucked down tight against the glass rim. *Ping.* The wedge of light recedes with the sun into the horizon. And later another ping, and then much later, the kitchen clean and settled into dark, Bill and I sitting in the living room, the final ping. It comes to me through the conversation of the television the way the clock at my grandmother's came to me through my dreams, striking the hour even in the darkest of the night.

Everyone Talks about It

Elnora Bixby

How do you start a conversation in Hawaii? That is, after you've said "aloha." The climate there is always what we would consider perfect. There are no extremes of temperature and no seasons except in name only. I talked to a man last week whose two sons had both been stationed in Hawaii during their military service. Both of them wanted to get back to more inhospitable climates; they didn't like the monotony of the always perfect weather.

I've never heard that complaint around here. We are so accustomed to inclement weather that without it we would be struck mute most of the time. We surely would never know how to start a casual conversation.

We have so many choices here that it is almost a miracle if we get past the weather report. Tell me if you haven't heard any of these: Hot enough for you? Cold enough for you? Did it freeze at your place last night? How much rain did you get? Did the hail do any damage around your place? Any trees blow over in the wind? There must have been a tornado last night. Did you hear how it rained during the night? Were you snowbound? How long did it take be-

fore you could get out? Did the electricity go off in the storm? We
had forty-two below at our place this morning. The rain ruined the
entire crop; I can't even get in to harvest it. The pipes froze and
flooded the basement. Any bridges washed out down your way?
Can you get in the fields yet? Did you get your crop in/out before
the rains started? Have you had to water your garden? Is it frozen
enough in the woods to get your wood out? It was too stormy to go
fishing; we couldn't even launch a boat. The hail ruined our roof.

I suppose I missed a few weather-related conversation openers.
We certainly have many options. Heat and cold, rain and snow,
sunshine and clouds. I suppose that is why we treasure the perfect
days so much. We are in no danger of monotonous weather.

But a strange thing happens in climates such as ours. We live
longer. North Dakota residents live even longer than we do in Minnesota, and their weather is even more perverse than ours. The
people who study these statistics believe the changeable weather
adds to our longevity. The constant adjustment our bodies must
make to the changing temperatures keeps them more fit, just as
exercise keeps our muscles in good shape.

I must admit there are some days I would be willing to sacrifice a
day or two of life to have better weather, but now that I don't have
to drive in the worst of it, I can even enjoy some of the storms.

Mark Twain's famous comment that everyone talks about the
weather but nobody does anything about it is still true. So keep
the long johns for the cold, the shorts for the heat, a hard hat for
hail, and an umbrella for rain. In this country we need them all.
Don't forget the snow shovel, and plug in the head bolt heater.

How's the weather out your way?

I hate you, northern Minnesota! You are a treacherous friend. I
have loved you, praised you, sounded like a travel brochure for
you, and how do you repay me? With the coldest, snowiest, most
miserable, cantankerous, most horrible weather of the century,
that's how. You couldn't give me a nice late fall and early winter to

finish up my driving-to-work career, could you? I would have been so kind to you if you had done that, but you double-crossed me. You didn't miss a thing. I have been snowbound. I have played snowplow with a car that was meant for paved roads and the balmy breezes. I had a battery die in the middle of the road—"deader'n a nit," to use my husband's expression. I have had to be towed home, and though I appreciated the tow, I am terrified of the experience and I'm still shaking.

Oh sure, the snow has drifted so it looks like sculptured marble, the pine trees look as if they had tons of white icing poured on them, the full moon makes the outdoors breathtakingly beautiful. That's great stuff for January—we can handle it then. We expect cold weather, deep snow, and ridiculous wind chill factors then, but when you do it in November and December it ain't funny and it ain't fair. We have enough to contend with with the shrinking daylight hours and steeling ourselves for the winter. This is taking advantage of our tolerance for abuse in the wintertime. It's no wonder the dinosaurs said the heck with it and gave up the battle. There are times when I feel as if I'm slated to be the next dinosaur.

I've tried to accommodate you with the wool and goose down clothing and the sheepskin boots, but you are so unforgiving. Forgetting a measly snow shovel can mean the difference between making it or not making it to a destination. Where is your tolerance and understanding for poor judgment and bad memory? By the time I have remembered everything, you'll warm up again, and I'll be an overdressed pessimist with a snow shovel and no snow to shovel.

Some poet, a long time ago, said, "If winter comes, can spring be far behind?" You bet it can, and especially this year.

I have just driven through the month of January again. I hope it will be the last time. I plan to be home in January next year. Driving has been a mini-education that was not covered in the written exam.

I have learned to stay on the road when fresh snow has obliterated all signs of where it is. I've learned to drive on ice—don't brake, don't change the speed, and don't drop the clutch suddenly if you downshift. I have straightened out of skids without going in the ditch while saying to myself, "When they say to steer into a skid, and the front end is going one direction and back end is going the other, which direction is into?" And I still don't know. I know that getting flat tires sounds like having a tired owl in the backseat. I can, if I have to, find the dipstick. I know that when I am home and the gas gauge needle is on E (as in empty) I can still drive eighteen miles to the nearest filling station, if I don't speed and am lucky. I know that when you meet a car on a narrow gravel road, there's a fine line between far enough and too far over to the side. I have learned to beware of the car snatcher that lurks beside the gravel roads. If you look for him in the woods beside the road, he will grab the car and make it leave erratic tracks, or leave you sitting helplessly in a ditch or a snowbank.

But I will miss driving to work every day. Not the icy roads, or the cold, or the blizzards, but it has its rewards. During the fifteen years I have driven to work, I have seen things I would not have seen from my windows at home. I have watched the years progress in the measured rhythm from snow to flooded fields to early green through golden fields and harvest and snow again.

I have seen a deer with her fawns following behind, crossing the road at the same place, until I feel as if I should know their names, they are so familiar. There was a family of moose that I used to see, the bull, cow, and calf. A bald eagle beside the road, so big that I drove for a couple of miles in sheer astonishment at its size before I reacted to the fact that I had just seen my first bald eagle.

The chartreuse shade of new leaves, and finding out that the same areas leaf out first each year. A mallard taking flight from a roadside ditch, with the sun shining on the droplets falling away, turning them golden. Pelicans flying, gleaming white in the sun, and, as if on signal, all of them bank and turn, and soar. Sandhill cranes patrolling a field where they must have a nest. Black ravens, bobbing and hopping as they fly over a dead animal on the road. Seagulls covering the fields and roads, waiting for the last second before they fly. Small, fat black and white ducks swimming in Bostic Creek. A pair of beavers walking on their hind legs, plodding across the road, looking like a tired old couple coming home from a hard day's work, with their stooped shoulders, their clumsy walk, and their broad flat tails dragging behind them like an empty gunny sack.

The color change of grass and foliage and flowers. Bright yellow cowslips to announce spring's arrival. Lavender fireweed and orange Indian paintbrush. Pink and white lady's slippers clustered in bunches in late June. Queen Anne's lace and joe-pye weed in July. Black-eyed Susans smiling in the summer sun. Maple turning red, poplars turning yellow, and tamaracks like a bright exclamation point in the fall.

And in the short December days, the yard lights gleaming to mark the houses in the country, until I see the last one, and I'm home again, driving under the light and into the garage.

I'll miss it. Not all of it, but there are the moments.

It's dreaming time again, a time when we begin to dream about what we'll do next spring and summer. We have a list so long we'd have to live in a southern climate to accomplish it all between last snow and first snow, but at this time of the year it all seems possible.

One thing occupying our mind right now is the garden. The seed catalogs have arrived, the picture of succulent produce has us anxious to begin, and our hopes are buoyed up with their literature. We not only forget our short summers and our failures, but also forget that we are not crazy about beets, we hate to shell peas, and we don't even have the best soil. Our soil is so bad it needs to be fertilized to make quack grass grow. On my first attempt to raise a garden, the only thing that gave me my seed back was potatoes. I grew one potato under each hill.

We moved the garden to a different spot and fertilized with old manure. We almost had a good garden that year, but the animals—wild, unseen, and unidentified—ate it faster at night than we could eat it in the daytime. So we built a fence and put on more manure. It kept the animals out and produced a bumper crop of weeds. It is the sort of garden now where we hope our visitors (a) don't ask to see the garden (it's embarrassing) or (b) don't have a garden of their own so, in comparison, ours looks good.

But as usual, at this time of the year, we're planning on a great garden again. Drawing plans, making lists, and discussing whether or not to invest in a garden tiller. We can come up with a reason for every dollar the tiller costs. Talking compost, peat, and fertilizer, turning the soil over in our minds more often than we'll actually do it next summer. If our interest or enthusiasm flags, we have only to look at the catalog, and we're believers again.

Tell me we'll never get as much produce from our garden for the rest of our lives as the tiller costs. Tell me that for what the two of us use, we could get it more easily from a neighbor with his surplus. Tell me the rains will come at the wrong time, and we will not get it watered soon enough in the dry periods. Tell me everything will ripen on Monday, and by Saturday, when I have time to take care of it, it will be over the hill. Deep down, I know all these things, but when I look at those beautiful seed catalogs, I don't really believe it.

Right now, I believe we'll have garden produce as beautiful to look at, and much better to eat, than those pictures. And right now I believe the radishes will not all mature the same day, and then go to seed. The tomatoes will all ripen on the vine, the broccoli will not get worms, the corn will be sweet and tender and will not blow over in the wind, the melons will be the right size when I am ready to take care of them, the lettuce will be crisp and crunchy, and the flowers will bloom, adding beauty to our Eden. Right now, in February, I believe all that.

Ah, but then there's September, and the dreaming days will be over.

Finally I have been rewarded for all the bad roads and storms I went through my working years, and for the days I stayed home with a guilty conscience because I couldn't get through the roads. Wednesday was the first day since my retirement when the roads were blocked so completely even the mail couldn't get through. We stayed snugly snowbound and loved it.

Actually, I loved it more than my husband did. He didn't have the backlog of bad driving conditions that I had, and he was the one who would be cleaning the snow away when it was all over. But even he got caught up in the spirit of the storm.

Fortunately, we had warning of the storm so we were able to get prepared for it. He went to town early in the morning to get groceries and an extension cord to use on the snow blower to start it. He got home early enough, with no storm, so we began to wonder if we were going to miss the storm. But it came.

I was waiting for this day. I knew what a good snowbound day needs: a good book, good food, and a warm fire. These are just the basics; add your own requirements.

I had a good book—a huge one, eight hundred pages long—just the right kind. An interesting one but not with a plot so gripping that it can't be laid down. The kind of book that is taken in sips rather than gulped down.

A good storm requires baking. Not only to give the house a warm feeling, but for the smells of cooking to impart the feeling of sustenance and well-being. Fresh-baked bread or soup, cooked all day long, or something that has a particular comforting smell will do it. I didn't want to raise expectations too high so I would be expected to do it every storm, so I settled for only two of the three. I made soup and apple pie. That was enough to make the house smell like a haven from the storm.

In order to enjoy a storm one needs a safe, sheltered feeling. I don't know why popcorn fits the need, but somehow munching popcorn and reading a book does just that. And warmth. A storm really needs a fireplace with sight and sound of crackling wood, but a fireplace is a fickle friend in our climate, so just hearing the furnace go on now and then was enough.

At our place we need a couple of other things as well. Birds at the feeder to remind us there are other living things that need sustenance during a storm, and the promise of watching them come and go as the storm progresses. So I carried out a refill of seeds to make sure there would be enough to last through the storm.

And at our house a storm needs cribbage. The first time we were snowbound we spent three days without electricity, which certainly limited our choices. We played cribbage because our only deck of cards was three cards short. We never checked to see which were missing, but we spent a lot of time counting fifteen-two, fifteen-four before the storm was over. It has become a tradition, since that, to always play cribbage in a storm. We play now with a full deck, or at least we tell ourselves that.

So the snow quit and the winds died down, and only the cleanup remained. I should apologize to everyone who had to be out in the storm, but age—like rank—has its privileges.

It's coming again. Crow Winter.

I've watched for it every year since I was a little girl, that last brief gasp of winter before true spring. I used to fight the inevitable, thinking that surely we would miss it one year.

I was still young enough to feel the freshness of the world—as if it had all been spread out for my benefit—when I first heard the term *Crow Winter.*

I had come racing to find my father to tell him the news. "Spring is here! I saw a whole flock of crows!"

I had to tell my father first. Who else was so awestruck by nature? He had shown me the difference between spruce and balsam. He'd pointed out the polar star and told me how to find it by sighting along the Big Dipper. He'd dig in the damp leaf mold with me to find wild ginger blossoms. "Cup and saucer," he called them. He touched the lady's slippers gently and reverently. He'd awakened me once to watch the northern lights dance in the sky one brilliant winter night.

So I fully expected him to be as excited as I about spring. Instead, he rubbed the top of my head and said, "Spring isn't really here yet. We still have to have Crow Winter. We always have another little bit of snow after the crows come back."

I was startled. What rash superstition was this? Next he'd be planting by the moon.

"That's not really true," I protested. "Why should it happen like that?"

"The crows are like you. They're too impatient for spring. You go barefooted too soon; they come back too soon."

I still wasn't convinced. "This year will be different. You'll see."

"All right," he said, "the first year we don't have Crow Winter, you come and tell me about it."

So I have been waiting to tell him he was wrong. At first eagerly. Later I told my children, so they could watch too. And my grandchildren will watch, too. I shall pass it on like a legacy.

I have waited and watched for more than forty years. But I waited too long to say I was wrong. Each year, like the rallying cry of a baseball team, I said, "Wait until next year." I waited, and his eyes became dim, and he no longer knew which of his children I was. I waited, and his skin took on the transparency of approaching death.

Yesterday, as we stood in the cemetery and the sun shone on all his children and grandchildren and great-grandchildren, the crows flew over us, cawing loudly. But this time I know there will be a Crow Winter. And today I have a new granddaughter born. I will tell her, too, about trees and butterflies, and flowers, and northern lights. And Crow Winter.

Solid Winter

Jana Studelska

I live here for the summers.

For those few, precious days when the pine needles sizzle in the sun, when I can smell the hot pitch through the screen windows as I lie reading on a cotton blanket. For the cold blue cords of spring water that wrap up the sides of my brown body and then weightlessly pop me to the lake surface at the edge of my father's gray cedar dock. For the pink evenings of June, when the light in the western sky seems barely to have left before it has run all the way around the planet and is singing again in the east. For the thick, humid afternoons and the deep thunder that follows, and the shattering stillness as the clouds pull away from the rinsed air.

But it is the winter that defines my life, the winter that determines the parameters of my being and the geology of my years. My whole history is in chapters held together with bookends of winter seasons. I struggle with winter, lean against it, push my way through it. I wallow, sleep, read, chap, shelter, and slip underneath its weight, underneath its indifferent, distant light. I am afraid that if I let it, winter would casually, violently bury me, like a grinding glacier.

It is through this struggle that I find my sense, my order.

On winter mornings, the dark sky and I hurl dark accusations back and forth. Morning, I recite to the sun, does not begin until it is light enough to distinguish a dog from a tree stump at a distance. I get up anyway, according to my clock, and I wait for the sun to appear over the jagged ripsaw pines south of town. It rolls up the sides of my dining room wall, then down the neighbor's brick wall, just peeking over the southern rim of sky. I drink coffee and wait. In winter I wait.

While it is light, I go into the woods, wandering through the snow-covered trees, in the thick deep drifts, breathing the coldest air, deep into my lungs where it expands again. I want to see the length of the shadows and listen to the chickadees, clipped sideways to alder brush just feet from where I walk, singing winter songs under black caps. I gasp for light, drowning at the solstice, proud of my suffering. I have to absorb light, even as it is mediated by reflection off snow, so that I don't dwindle into just flesh. I am proud to know this, after many winters. I have earned this knowledge.

In winter, my body pales, like a camouflage. My hands bleed at the woodpile. My skin dries and flakes like sugar cookie dough. I am lumpy and misshapen in thick sweaters, hidden under my own winter blankets.

In my mind, even on the coldest days, I can still reason; this is what makes me human. Yet each winter I face the same truth: this season cannot exercise logic, but nonetheless its logic overpowers my humanness. The winter contracts me into an appropriate size. It blows through my routines, shortstops my commitments, demands that I simply pay attention to what is bigger than me. My reason and logic are my hobbies in deep winter, not marketable skills. I concede. I am a pacifist.

I never demonstrate determination like November. I am never bigger than December. I never feel as strong as January. I cannot endure like February. I cannot stretch as far as March. I cannot lie with such conviction as April. I am not as hopeful as May snow. I am reminded that I have far to go.

On winter evenings, my fires are always red and orange and blue, each color succeeding the other as the fuel turns from birch to oak. I hopefully bargain harder wood for a longer fire. When the red color deep in my firebox is the same color as the red dusk deep in the southern sky, and both appear at the same time as supper cooks on the stove, I know that the cold winter will have to wait outside tonight.

Later, the winter and I battle silently under heavy strata of wool and feathers. I stuff my cats like hot potatoes under the covers. I wear slippers to bed, only to wake later in a furious sweat. I cover the window next to my bed with my extra pillows, but later pull them to me for the shock of their cold slap. I am always soothed.

In winter I examine my most humiliating traits. I grow tired of my bad habits, bored with my own excuses. I quit television, I lose weight, I vacuum walls, I start writing novels and stitching hopelessly intricate needlepoint patterns. The strength of my resolution is second only to weariness of my own bad company. I am always a better person after winter, because I know what makes me ugly and I have faced it.

In the spring, when winter recedes, when the glacier moves the bulk of ten thousand years backward one more time, I am different because of it. The light widens the days and threatens to wrap around the clock and drive me mad with the smell of melted earth and the sight of fat, sticky buds. I drag what's left of me up to the surface, to the edge, from where I scurry into a seed catalog, and daringly cast my eyes toward a red canoe.

It is perhaps these simple spring steps that make my winter solid. The sudden brazenness of my courage, the lusty want for thawed garden soil. It is only when I can fall blindly forward into summer, bare arms flung to the side, eyes wide open, that I know what winter has done.

And I am grateful.

THE LIVES AROUND US

Chickadee Bob

Peter M. Leschak

Change, of course, can be traumatic. Bob, for instance, lost his tail.
It was on a November fourth. I remember because I was helping
our friend Rastus secure his boat for the winter. It got down to nine
degrees that morning, and there was a rim of ice around the lake.
In two weeks there would be one great sheet, and the lake would
be sealed for five months.

We dragged the sixteen-foot Lund far up onto the shore, flipped
it over, and chained it to a birch. It was sad duty. The aluminum
hull was crusted with frost, the anchor rope frozen stiff. Wasn't it
only yesterday that the seats were warmed by June sunshine and
smelled like minnows? I recalled towing a heavy stringer of small-
mouth bass. But like the black bears, fishing boats must hibernate.
It's just a pity they don't produce offspring while they're at it.

When we returned to the cabin, it was to a scene of high drama.
Pam and I had recently begun filling our bird feeder with sun-
flower seeds. We do business from late October to late March, and
our yard luckily becomes a hangout for jays, grosbeaks, and black-
capped chickadees. They literally flock in.

But there's a flip side to this lavish welfare program. At least once or twice a week a bird wings straight into one of our windows. We hear a loud, flat *thunk!* and know that yet another of our clients has executed a flying body slam against the glass. I guess they're fooled by reflections of trees and sky. We rush to the window to see if there's been a casualty. Occasionally a bird is killed—usually a bigger one, such as a pine grosbeak. However, most of the time they're okay, startled and mortified, no doubt, but able to fly away from it. Some do better than others.

We still chuckle about one punch-drunk chickadee. Pam saw it hit the west window and then immediately flit over to a nearby aspen. It perched on one of the lower branches, apparently all right. But as Pam watched, it began to nod and weave. It struggled mightily to remain conscious, repeatedly jerking its little head back from the brink—as if it were last call down at the tavern. But finally the concussion triumphed. The chickadee passed out and fell forward. Pam prepared to run out and retrieve it, but the bird never left the perch. Its tiny talons had locked onto the branch, and it simply swung back and forth beneath the limb, like a feathery pendulum. It hung there for a few moments and then came to. It hoisted itself erect and flew off—a live presentation of Looney Tunes.

Well, on that chilly November morning another black-capped chickadee had pounded into a window—this one on the east side. Pam hurried to the door and found the stunned bird crouched on the top step. In another moment it would have been a quivering tidbit for the Reverend, our dog, but Pam scooped it up and brought it inside.

She cuddled it for a few minutes, afraid it was going to expire anyway. She opened her palms to take a peek, and the chickadee burst out of her cupped hands and flew wildly around the living room.

Rastus and I arrived to see Pam standing on the sofa, gingerly reaching up to where the bird had perched on a beam. Bloody

Alice, our cat, was also on the sofa, watching the proceedings with great interest. Pam made a gentle thrust, but the chickadee was off, fluttering against the tops of the windows.

I grabbed Alice and, despite ill-natured protests, put her outside. I then went upstairs to the bathroom and a moment later I heard Pam scream—and Rastus laugh. I hastened back down and found Pam clutching a small bouquet of feathers.

"Its tail came off!" she cried.

The chickadee had paused on the beam again, and instead of trying to collar the entire bird, Pam thought it would be more efficient to just pinch the tail feathers. She could then quickly cup her other hand around its pinioned body. But apparently this was an old trick used by shrikes, cats, and other predators, and the chickadee was ready with an automatic defense mechanism. It issued a loud squeak and violently beat its little wings. The tail feathers slipped out, jettisoned between Pam's fingers, and the now-stubby bird flew off.

Pam was horrified, but she finally recaptured the chickadee by throwing a dish towel over it. Tail or no, it would have to go back out into the early-winter world. But surely its tail feathers weren't expendable. We supposed this handicap would lessen its chances of survival in some way. We had read that up to 50 percent of the chickadee population dies every winter, and that in order to survive, they must feed almost constantly during the abbreviated daytime. This means a lot of flitting and flying, and presumably a raft of tail feathers is an important part of the operation. Thus, even though the chickadee flew away from the house with no apparent difficulty—and some obvious relief—we were sorrowful. Its days were probably numbered. Pam felt guilty.

And sure enough, the bird disappeared. Dozens of chickadees worked our feeder every day, from dawn till dusk, but they all had tails. We had expected the worst but were surprised the injured bird had gone so quickly. Over the next three months, as the woods filled with snow and bitterly cold air descended from Canada, Pam would often mention the hapless chickadee—regret mixed with a shred of hope. I would say yes, it was too bad, but the bird was certainly long dead, and that was the way of the forest, the survival of the fittest, et cetera, et cetera.

But on the morning of January 28, I heard Pam squeal, and then shout, "He's back! He's back!"

She had been watching the brisk activity at the feeder when a chickadee with no tail flew in and started pecking at the seeds. Pam was overjoyed, convinced that this was the bird whose tail she'd ripped out in November.

We immediately christened it Bob, reflecting both its tailless state and our strange presumption that the bird was male. I suppose we've been conditioned to associate injury, grim endurance, and survival with the males of the various species—forgetting all about pregnancy, for example. (When Pam caught herself making a chauvinistic assumption she noted that a creature who had unwittingly dived into a closed window, and then lost its tail through an unnecessary act of bravado, was surely male.)

For the next month Bob was at the feeder almost every day, crunching seeds with the best of them. In effect he was a tagged animal, the only chickadee distinctive enough to be considered an individual. We could follow his patterns of daily activity, unconfused by the usual isomorphic nature of chickadeehood. I had often tried to focus on a single bird, but with a dozen clones coming and going at a furious clip, I would lose track of my subject almost immediately.

But Bob stood out, and we noted that he seemed to go at the feeder in two shifts. For an hour or so each morning, and then again in the afternoon, he'd be out there hustling for seeds. Where he'd spend the rest of the working day we didn't know. Perhaps he was out eating what chickadees would naturally eat if there were no feeder. In any case, if his behavior was typical, then we were probably seeing a lot more chickadees in the course of a day than we'd suspected, for it's literally impossible to glance at the feeder at any given moment and not see a chickadee. A frenetic shift is always on duty.

At the beginning of March, Pam noticed that Bob's tail seemed to be growing back. It was becoming a little difficult to pick him out from the rest of the flock. He disappeared again, and we worried. But then, in mid-March, a chickadee zoomed in to the feeder sporting a full-length, pure-white tail. A normal black-capped chickadee's tail is gray. It had to be Bob. His resurgent feathers were a badge of honor and success; he was a hero.

We were pleased, but surprised. Back in November I wouldn't have bet a nickel on the wintertime chances of a chickadee with no tail feathers. But it was Aesop who said, "It is not only fine feathers that make fine birds."

A Parliament of Owls

John Henricksson

Chances are still good that any one of us, at some dark midnight
hour, may be suddenly awakened by a quavery owl cry and feel an
inexplicable shiver no conscious thought could have summoned.
If the shiver is followed by a strange longing to see the crier
and know more of its mysterious ways, then you have a right to
suspect that some trace of owl witchcraft lives among us.
VIRGINIA HOLMGREN, in *Owls in Natural History*

Barred owls, birds of mystery and the deep silences, are our evanes-
cent companions in this old forest. Likely because of its nocturnal
habits, unblinking stare, and weird night noises that penetrate sleep
and log walls, the barred owl remains a spectral presence, making
its legendary role as death messenger, or omen of tragedy, seem
quite believable.

At the Gunflint cabin we often hear its doleful requiem during
the wilderness night but seldom are aware of it during daylight
hours. Last year a barred owl visited us regularly in the afterglow
of the westering sun and gave us a rare glimpse of its menacing
company.

Next to the dock an old white cedar clings tenaciously to the slabby granite boulders along the shore, gnarled roots coiling and grasping holds in the fissured rocks. It slants out at a forty-five-degree angle to the water's surface, flat green sprays still growing at midtrunk, but the gray, weathered, and branchless tip points out over the water directly at the North Star like a warrior's lance. Each evening the barred owl glided in silently and perched at the end of the snag, watching the water below and casting an ominous shadow on the flotillas of young mallards and mergansers being shepherded to nighttime coves by nervous mothers. We often wondered if this sinister bird could have been Oley, an orphaned barred owl raised by our neighbor, Peggy Heston, a tiny lady with a heart as big as a watermelon for the young of wild creatures.

Peggy had gone out to her mailbox one morning and found this frowzy little dirt-covered owlet squeaking in the gravely row of scrapings the road grader leaves on the shoulder. At first she thought it might have fallen from a nest as owlets frequently do because the adults are such slovenly nest builders. In fact, most of the time they use the tattered remains of other birds' nests. Peggy thought that if she left the owlet there, the mother owl might come and reclaim it, but when she went back in an hour it was still there looking more bedraggled and forlorn than ever. She scooped it up in her apron and carried it back to her kitchen, where it perked up considerably after a substantial breakfast of chopped eggs, hamburger, and milk. She named him Oley and he quickly adapted to the good life at Peggy's. He spent many hours watching television from a perch on the back of the davenport. When he got a little bigger, Peggy made him a sturdy roost, which was a little higher so he would be safe from the dog, whom he delighted in terrorizing with sudden bizarre screeches.

Peggy kept Oley around the house for almost a year, although she knew that someday she would have to return him to the wild. She was concerned that the lifestyle he had become used to would spoil him and prevent him from working for a living, so in the spring she began his on-the-job training by dragging a stuffed mouse around the grass on a string. At first Oley thought this was a pretty dumb game and ignored the mouse, but his instincts were eventually aroused and gradually he began to get the idea, pouncing on the mouse and literally tearing the stuffing out of it. After several mouse replacements, Peggy decided Oley was ready for his finals. She took him out into the woods, released him from his tether, and went back to the house to worry about his chances of making it on his own after the epicurean life he had been leading.

About eight o'clock that evening Peggy was startled by a commotion at the front screen door. When she went down to investigate, there perched on the railing was Oley, fanning his wings against the door and holding a deer mouse in his talons. We aren't supposed to believe that creatures can communicate with us, but it would be hard to convince Peggy that Oley wasn't telling her, "See, Ma. I can do it."

Perhaps its phantomlike reputation has developed because the owl is heard more often than it is seen. Its ability to remain motionless for hours and its elegant camouflage of gray, brown, buff, and black baffles even the most careful observer. And it has other tricks of concealment that often bewilder me even when I am certain there is a barred owl nearby. One of the most disconcerting is its ability to literally become a part of another object.

Every mature forest has an abundance of snags, the ghostly trunks of standing dead trees, broken off by wind or lightning, stripped of bark and silvery with age. Many are spiraled with shelf fungus and dappled with the holes of cavity-nesting birds. The barred owl finds the notchy tops of these snags perfect observation posts where its mottled coat and blocky shape blend it into an upward extension of the trunk. There it sits, statue-still and unseen until it suddenly glides off, pouncing on a scurrying vole or snatching a woodpecker off a nearby tree.

Hiking on the Loon Lake portage road one August morning filling my bucket with the plump raspberries of late summer, I stopped to eat my lunch seated in a natural armchair formed by the up-turned roots of a windthrow, the exposed and contorted roots of a fallen white pine. Looking around absently in the moss nearby, I began to notice a number of owl pellets—the dried up and regurgitated remains of bones, fur, and other indigestibles owls cough up and scatter near their roosts and hidey-holes. Because owls have no teeth, they cannot chew their food. They tear it into chunks or swallow it whole. The materials their body cannot digest are packed with a mucous in their stomachs and then up-chucked. When I noticed several of these pellets near the snag, I got up, stepped a few feet away, and searched closely. Sure enough, there right at the top of the snag was a barred owl, wings slightly drooped over the broken top of the snag. Only the unblinking gaze of its molasses-colored eyes gave it away. The eyes are the quickest and most accurate field marking of the barred owl. All other owls here have lemon-yellow eyes. They are about the size of human eyes and can change focus rapidly, but can concentrate light with about a hundred times the ability of human eyes, allowing them to zero in on their prey instantly. Unique, fluffy feathers along the leading edge of their wings enable them to fly silently and strike without warning.

The northern barred owl (*Strix varia*) has several other distinguishing features that make it easy to identify. It is a big bird, fourth largest among the eighteen North American owl species, and has a vertically barred breast, a round, tuftless head, and very large ear cavities, which give it the keenest hearing of any bird. Allan Eckert reported a barred owl that could hear a mouse running on hard-packed earth fifty yards away.

But it is the voice, an exceptional voice, that gives it away even in the dark of night. The most familiar call is the four rapidly repeated *hoo*'s, which sound remarkably like "Who cooks for you?" But it has a variety of other sounds and phrasings, the most startling of which—a bloody-murder sound that mimics a woman screaming—is heard during the late-winter mating. It can also hiss, chuckle, growl, and groan. One of my birding friends has her own voice identification formula: "If it sounds like nothing else on earth," she says, "it's a barred owl."

They fare well here in this forest. Voles, shrews, deer mice, passerine birds, and an occasional snowshoe hare are on the daily menu, but consistent with its other eccentricities, it might wade a stream for frogs or even kill and eat a skunk because it has no sense of smell.

Another owl neighbor, far more delightful than the solemn barred owl, is a tiny clown, the saw-whet owl (*Aegolius acadicus*). The common name sounds inappropriate now, but it came originally from the loggers who thought its monotonous, scraping voice sounded like the whetting, or sharpening, of a large mill saw. I prefer its baptismal species name, given for the region of its first documentation, Nova Scotia. Its tedious, mechanical call is often repeated a hundred times a minute, and local birders have more appropriate descriptions of it, including a truck's backup signal, or a spaceship in a swamp.

Just before leaving for the cabin one morning, I got a call from Orv Gilmore, who lives nearby, telling me to bring some batteries for my smoke alarm system. Its constant beeping, which signals weakening batteries, was keeping him awake. When I arrived, Orv was gone, but there was a note tacked on the door: "Sorry about the false alarm. The beeping turned out to be a lovesick saw-whet owl in the big cedar tree near the woodshed."

The owl's reputation for solemnity could not have been based on the behavior of the saw-whet. It is the most entertaining creature in the forest, and boreal show biz is its natural venue. One of its acts is a soft-shoe dance in which it hops up and down a branch, first on one foot, then the other, and it can turn its face upside down. Most owls can turn their heads 180 degrees so fast it looks as though they are turning their heads completely around. The saw-whet turns its head over instead of sideways—it's the only owl that does this. It is disconcerting to be focusing a camera or field glasses on one and suddenly discover its face is on upside down, the beak up near the top of its head and the eyes near its breast. It is also an accomplished ventriloquist, which makes it very difficult to locate. Even while you're staring at it, perched at the rim of its hole or in a thick bush near the ground, the voice will come from high up in the tree. It has virtually no tail, a seven-inch body, and a somewhat misshapen head, giving it a disproportionate, buffoonish appearance. Because the wing beats alternate, flight is erratic, setting it off on a staggering flight path. A thoroughly enchanting little bird.

Recently we learned there is another owl here, but we have never seen it. It is the boreal, or Richardson's, owl (*Aegolius funereus*). The voyageurs gave it the liltingly beautiful French-Canadian name "la nyctale boréale"—the night owl of the north—and the Montagne Indians of the far north called it the "water dripping bird," referring to its ascending, liquid song, which is heard only on spring nights during the mating season. Research biologist Bill Lane tells us that is why we have never seen it. "Boreals are strictly night hunters," he says. "And the boreal's call, a twelve-note rising trill that resembles a jacksnipe's territorial flight call, is only heard at night in March and April, which reduces the likelihood of birders spotting it."

The boreal owl was discovered here by naturalist Kim Eckert in 1978, the first sighting in the lower forty-eight states. Not long after, Steve Wilson, a forest ecologist, stumbled over one while he was trout fishing on the Baptism River. Since then, both Lane and Wilson have covered many miles conducting listening post surveys and researching the elusive birds. Lane estimates there are about 220 singing males in this area. It may be possible I have seen one without recognizing it because the boreal is very similar in appearance to the saw-whet. The boreal is a little bigger, has a sooty facial ring, and has a yellow beak in contrast to the saw-whet's black beak.

There are other owls nearby in different habitats: cleared land, newer forest growth, and areas closer to Lake Superior where more moderate winter temperatures reduce the snow depth, making hunting easier. In these areas are the aggressive great horned owl; the great gray owl, largest of the North American owls with its sixty-inch wingspan; the hawk owl with its black sideburns and rounded, falconlike tail. Farther north in the tundra country are the regal Arctic snowy owls, who sometimes migrate here in winter when the prey population crashes in their stark homeland, and the secretive long-eared owl, a dweller in the lonely spruce and tamarack lowlands.

"Night bird, death bringer, have you come for me?" asks Grandmother as Virginia Holmgren begins her fascinating tales of owl legends and folklore. Sir Edmund Spenser called the owl "death's dread messenger," and most American Indian tribes believed the owl was present at death and accompanied the departed on their last journey. During the Renaissance, artists often placed an owl on Calvary's cross in crucifixion paintings, and even the august science of taxonomy carries fragments of legend in their genus and species names for owls: *Strix* (Latin) and *Striga* (Greek) both mean witch, or hag. The American hawk owl is *Surnia*, bird of ill-omen, and the boreal is *funereus*, the funeral bird.

Why should all this mournful, dolorous symbolism be laid on the owl? Why the age-old association with death and tragedy? I suspect it is because most owls, except the silly saw-whet, are ideal metaphors for fear. They are mysterious and unknowable. They strike swiftly and silently with rapier talons. They make strange, haunting noises in the night that seem to come from shadow worlds, and their empty, inscrutable stare impales the imagination. Also, they have been around for years beyond counting, 50 million at least, in the same form. Every people in every culture have had owls among them, so the stories have had centuries to simmer in the juices of uneasy imaginations.

Of course, side by side with the frightening images are those of wisdom and sagacity. Those perceptions are why we call the group a "parliament" of owls, and we owe that mythology to Athena, the Greek goddess of wisdom, whose constant companion and adviser was a little round-headed owl.

The stories go on and on. Folklore is the vehicle and the result of the oral tradition's passage through generations . . . telling and retelling the indigenous stories. Along the way new creatures and new events work their way into the fabric of the stories, and so I think again about Oley and his stuffed mouse and the clownish little saw-whet. Maybe someday they will star in stories about how the barred owl learned to hunt and the saw-whet owl made the forest laugh.

Wild Goose Chase

Jane Whitledge

Every autumn I look up at southbound flocks of geese with a mild feeling of envy, wanting to soar away, to be bound for unknown lakes and ponds, secluded river bends, and wide lonely cornfields. I live in the north woods and spend much of my time in northern Minnesota's Boundary Waters Canoe Area wilderness with my husband, Doran. Yet even when we're paddling on a breathtaking northern lake in October, something about geese veeing overhead sets up a pensive yearning that perhaps has nothing to do with places.

But the day in late October when a lone snow goose flew over our Basswood Lake campsite, I felt only surprise. Several days had passed on the lakes without our sighting a single flock. We suspected all geese had finally packed out of the north and were perhaps by now over Iowa or viewing the Mississippi somewhere along the Missouri border.

But then—*whoosh!*—suddenly there was a goose. Astonished, Doran and I looked up from our afternoon tea. Just above the tree-tops over our heads a lone snow goose flew, neck straight out, wings stroking hard, shrill fretful voice gabbling in alarm. And no wonder—right behind the goose followed two bald eagles, huge wings fanning the air confidently, in hot pursuit.

The chase took them over a bluff and out of sight, just up from camp. Shortly, a third eagle glided into view, circling the sky high over the bluff.

While we watched, this eagle folded its wings in close, dropped its feet like landing gear, and plummeted dramatically down through the air. I thought of Tennyson's eagle: *And like a thunderbolt he falls.* Somewhere up among the pines on the bluff, our eagle disappeared.

Curious to see what might be happening, we scrambled below into the hollow between camp and the bluff, breaking through naked hazel, dogwood, alder, and small birch. Sunny-yellow leaves scuffled pleasantly underfoot, and soon we were climbing the rocky side of the bluff.

I had never associated eagles with geese before. Eagles and osprey, yes; eagles and gulls, yes; eagles and fish, always. Many times we'd seen eagles filch fish from one of these birds, forcing gull or osprey to drop its catch, with the eagle zooming in to retrieve the stolen prize. Gulls and hawks chased eagles all spring, away from nests and young; loons wailed tremulously whenever eagles passed over a lake.

Hearts pounding, we reached the top of the bluff and looked around us. All was quiet—just scraggly, leafless sumac among the boulders and jack pine. We walked on, stopping when an eagle caught our eye as it lifted heavily from a pine branch and flew off alone. So the goose escaped, we thought, or was still fleeing the undaunted pair of eagles farther on.

We circled the hilltop. A cluster of pale corydalis bloomed from a crack near a boulder, delicate yellow and pink flower, complicated pale green leaves. Toughest of flowers, I thought, thriving from spring to fall in the most inhospitable nooks—flower I've come to love best in this rocky wilderness.

Already we were forgetting the snow goose. But then Doran pointed ahead to a mess of feathers. "The goose!" I said, hurrying to the place, noticing that it lay just below where the third eagle, probably too late for dinner, had launched. In the midst of all those gray and white feathers, softly propped in down, were the head, neck, and wings of the snow goose.

How quickly it was accomplished! Not more than fifteen minutes had passed since the goose and eagle had swooshed over our heads back in camp. Was this what I'd expected to see? Well, I should have guessed; it was simply that age-old routine: life and death, death and life, nature feeding on nature, and, ultimately, life going on.

Was this lone snow goose flying in a pattern with its flock when the eagles descended on it? And, we wondered, did eagles regularly pick migrating geese out of the air? Was this goose a solitary, vulnerable traveler? Was it sick or injured, and perhaps left behind to its fate?

Earlier that autumn, Doran woke me from half-sleep once, asking, "Hear the geese?"

I listened. On my back I gazed up at the tent, dreaming of geese passing over in the dark, the honking cries calling down to us, it seemed. We crawled outside; eyes straining skyward, we could only imagine all those wings working swiftly against the stars, an undulating vee navigating a route beneath the constellations. A jubilant passage.

Now I brushed the toe of my boot in the breeze-blown feathers, lifting one lifeless wing, my idea of a goose's life slightly altered.

In the Company of Wolves

Jim Brandenburg

Wildlife photography is always arduous work. It is sometimes lonely, and it is always intense. But some animals can be captured on film much more easily than others. Wolves present a particular set of problems, which is why most wolf photography is done with captive wolf packs placed in natural settings. Wolves are too wary to be fooled by common photographer tricks. Wolves on forested land take advantage of tree cover. They're secretive and mysterious, and their story is often revealed only by tracks in the snow. But it was my passion, or perhaps my obsession, to photograph wolves in the woods, so I had long thought about how to tell their story.

I had once spent the better part of a winter in the Minnesota wilderness in an attempt to photograph wolves. Even with the support of the U.S. Forest Service, which had flown me and my two months' worth of camping supplies into a territory where three packs roamed, I was unable to produce even one bad photograph. That particular approach was prone to failure. But a new method had since been forming in my mind.

I decided that the best approach would involve placing myself in the wolves' path, so to speak, as they made the rounds of their territory. With time, patience, and a good slice of luck, I ought to find myself in the right place from time to time. And I've always believed that you make your own luck through hard work. Ravenwood just might be the tool to help pull it off.

The land surrounding Ravenwood is some of the grandest country in the world, with thick, tangled forest and primordial bogs, all made penetrable by thousands of lakes linked by dozens of rivers. These waterways, whether navigated by canoe in the summer or crossed when frozen in the long winter, make travel possible.

The hills and valleys are covered with boreal forest. Dark pines, spruce, and fir spire toward the sky. Aspen, birch, and maple add their leafed diversity. Moose roam the woodland. At one time, woodland caribou fed in the jack pine forest and galloped across frozen lakes. And after timber barons stripped this area's tall pines, the second-growth forest attracted white-tailed deer.

Undoubtedly, wolves have been part of the region since this area was barely more than a rocky tundra growing in the wake of a slowly receding glacier. We know from archaeological sites that ancient humans, the Paleo-Indians, followed herds of caribou. It seems almost certain that wolves also feasted on that caribou flesh. As the land evolved into forest during the warmer ages that followed, wolves adapted too, stalking moose in the white winters and catching animals like beavers in the green summers.

Though more than half the virgin forest has been logged and the caribou are gone, the land surrounding Ravenwood represents the last vestiges of eastern forest. With a buffer of wilderness clear to the Arctic, the genetic artery of wildlife functions well. There may be more wolves in this region now than were here a hundred years ago. The newcomer white-tailed deer are probably more numerous than the caribou were. Since wolves don't much care what kind of venison they eat, they've done well by switching from one kind of deer to the other. And when the prey base grew, so did the number of wolves.

Other factors have contributed, of course. Wolves in Minnesota have been as persecuted and vilified as wolves elsewhere. A bounty on wolves existed as recently as 1965. Since 1967, the animals have been federally listed under the Endangered Species Act; in Minnesota, they are now considered a threatened species. Recent surveys indicate that their range has expanded to the south and west, proof they've responded to protection.

I chose the site for my Ravenwood cabin after much searching. I wanted a location that did not disrupt the functioning of the land and its wildlife, yet I needed to be situated at a spot where animals would be funneled directly toward me.

A small creek flows on the property. Creeks and rivers carve corridors along which wildlife travel. If prey travels through, so, eventually, will wolves. I doubt whether the water of this creek passes through any other spot as charming as the one where I chose to build. After hastening down a little rapids, the creek leaps over a twenty-foot waterfall, splashing noisily into the dark bowl below. As I scouted my new land, I found the beds of two moose along the bank nearby. I chose to build where the moose had slept, contouring the cabin into the hill stair-step fashion. Here the falls would drown out human noises and camera licks as I recorded the animal life around me.

A rock outcrop sits across the tiny valley of the creek, beneath towering white and Norway pines. By occasionally dragging road-killed animals to this spot, I hoped to encourage wolves to pause during their travels. I would do this sporadically, only in winter, and often not for months, for I did not want to condition the wolves to feeding here all the time, like garbage-dump bears. But if the wolves whose territory included Ravenwood found food here every once in a while, they would tend to remember. They might stop by when they passed through the area, especially if they always felt safe on my land.

Wolves are not to be unduly feared. There has been no verified attack on humans by a healthy wild wolf in North America. Not one. But even knowing this, it is hard to suppress the ancient flight reflex. I have felt that fear during the blue-black of a winter evening deep in the forest. The starkness of winter and the knowledge that everything in the frigid forest is eking out an existence makes the world seem scarier and more desperate. When I watch wolves rip apart a kill, when I see the power in their straining haunches and the terrible tearing teeth, I can imagine myself in the prey's position. But in all my wolf encounters, I've only felt threatened once, and in that instance I was at fault.

Several years ago, while I was working on a separate project to profile wolves in the high Arctic, I attempted to film a dominant male that had discovered a dead, beached seal. As the wolf ate, I sat frustrated because the entire scene was cast in shadows, and I knew my footage would be unusable. After a while, the wolf wandered off. I seized the opportunity, moved down to the carcass, and dragged it into the wonderful Arctic sunlight.

Preoccupied with my task, I was at first unaware that the wolf had returned. When I looked up, I was instantly frightened. I'd seen his aggressive posture when he dealt with other wolves, and I could tell he was unhappy with me for apparently trying to make off with his seal.

Every hair was erect on the wolf's back, and those on the back of my neck rose in response. Because wolves so readily read body language, I think they see our normal erect posture as a sign of dominance. But in this case I was crouched over the seal, a posture the wolf may have interpreted as submissive behavior. The wolf came running toward me, and I wasted no time in getting away, barely reaching my all-terrain vehicle in time. If I had stood my ground, though, I expect he would have backed off.

Clunk . . . clunk . . . Every fifteen seconds a pine cone dropped into my blind. I stared up at the red squirrel that was dropping the cones with annoying accuracy. A movement caught my eye and I turned to my task, which was watching a bear carcass that lay across the ravine from me. The ravens were getting excited. I didn't know how the bear had died. It might have been hit by a car on a nearby road, then crawled off to die. It was not killed by wolves, nor even visited by them. Not yet, at any rate. I watched patiently in the hope that the wolves would come.

Actually, I was confident they would come. The ravens had discovered the carcass the day before, and today they were already in the trees at dawn, when I awoke to resume my watch. By dark, no wolves had arrived, and I hoped they would stay away until the next day so I could photograph them. I busied myself at the cabin that evening, restless with anticipation.

Bernd Heinrich, who wrote a fascinating book called *Ravens in Winter* about raven research he conducted in Maine, found little correlation between the ravens' recruitment call (the "yell," as he called it) and the eventual arrival of predators. This surprised me. Ravens use the call to attract each other, but it is my feeling that they also call to attract predators—especially wolves—to unopened carcasses. I can only speculate that my experience is different from Heinrich's because wolves are not present in Maine, or because ravens relate differently to predators here than they do in Maine. But I have repeatedly seen wolves, as well as coyotes, come to a carcass shortly after it was discovered by yelling ravens.

The advantage for the ravens in this case, of course, was evident. With no means of penetrating the bear's thick skin, the ravens could not easily gain access to the meat.

Ravens on the ground always approach a carcass nervously, often "pogoing" into the air with a flap of their wings, as if to test whether the animal is truly dead, hoping to elicit a response if it is alive. I find a sense of braggadocio to some ravens' approach as they side-step up to the carcass in a nonchalant manner only to peck quickly, then jump away and strut. This behavior has occurred at every kill I've monitored, and it continues until the carcass is certified harmless by the settling in of one bold raven or by the presence of wolves. When the animal is verified dead, the entire flock moves in. I've seen as many as seventy ravens feeding on the same deer.

The efficiency of ravens at a carcass seems to encourage wolves to engorge themselves. Able to consume as many as twenty pounds at one meal—one quarter of their average weight—wolves take full advantage of their relatively infrequent meals. If they did not, they might return to a kill a few hours later to find that ravens and other scavengers had stripped it clean.

Dawn and the ravens both arrived, and I had a feeling from the start that this would be a big day.

A light snow begins to fall. There are ravens in the trees and on the ground, but none on the impenetrable carcass. Suddenly, as the pace of the snow quickens, those ravens on the ground fly into the trees. I look around.

A wolf has appeared on the ridge.

If I thought the ravens had been nervous, this wolf puts them to shame. It trots in cautiously, downwind of the bear, and crouches on its front paws. It repeatedly looks up at the ravens. Ever so slowly, the wolf works toward the bear, then finally gives it a timid nip before leaping back. The bear does not move. This encourages the wolf, which more boldly moves in for a second nip. Again, the bear does not move. The wolf looks up at the ravens, looks all around the forest, then takes a serious bite out of the bear. Like leaves falling from trees, the ravens tumble down to the bear.

The wolf grabs a chunk and steps back to eat it; then the ravens step onto the carcass and peck at the newly exposed flesh. This wolf is alone, but judging from its demeanor, I'd say it has good status within its pack. I think ravens have some understanding of wolf body language. Wolves that display clear dominance are pestered less often by the ravens, which sometimes dive bomb and peck wolves that seem submissive. The ravens peel back the bear's fatty skin, stuffing chunks of white fat into their beaks. As they clean the flesh, they tug the skin back, rolling it under their feet like we would roll up a carpet.

After wolves leave a carcass to stalk the quiet forest once again, a succession of creatures appears. Martens and fishers set upon clean ribs in order to chew leftover bits. Lushly coated foxes find fragments of food. Coyotes, which often bark in the distance until the wolves leave, sneak in for a snack. Eagles join the ravens in thoroughly stripping the carcass. Naked-headed turkey vultures show up for a meal. Hairy and downy woodpeckers trade birch trees for backbones. Even the flittering chickadees and the acrobatic nuthatches descend with the Canada jays for dinner.

Eventually, in spring, the mice, voles, insects, and microbes turn what is left of the carcass into new life. The enriched soil pushes up young growth that will one day be eaten by a deer, which will itself be eaten.

So, although ravens have a special relationship with the wolves, all of the forest occupants benefit from the chase and kill by the predators. This is the cornerstone of ecology—the understanding that, at some level, all creatures are dependent upon each other.

As I wander Ravenwood, I see such interdependencies occurring daily. We humans have witnessed these lessons since we first could think. We are not merely observers, but participants in the process. We benefit as each animal benefits. Despite all that we are, we remain part of the natural cycle. But too often, we forget.

The wolf has been our companion. And as a vital part of a fully functioning ecosystem, the wolf can serve as teacher, reminding us that two species sharing similar ecological niches might also share similar fates. If, one day, the wolf no longer finds the world a fit place in which to live, we may face a similar and inescapable destiny.

IN THE ELEMENTS

Sand Lake Peatland, October

Laurie Allmann

It was in Denmark, 1952. Saturday. The men were out in a bog near the village, cutting squares of peat to use as fuel to heat their homes, when they found the body. They cleared away the cold and sodden peat from around the head and shoulders, and then the legs, until the man was completely free from the bog. They saw that the body was hardly decomposed; he could not have been dead for long. A woman from the village said that she could identify the man. It was Red Christian, she said, a peat cutter she had known who had disappeared without a trace. Judging from the man's teeth, investigators estimated that he had been about thirty years old when he died. Then they ran a test, called radiocarbon dating, to find out how long ago he had died, how long he might have lain in the bog. The results of the test showed that the man had died more than sixteen hundred years ago. This was no Red Christian of modern-day Denmark. This was a man of the Iron Age.

Hitchcock at his best could not do better than the mysteries written over the centuries by the peatlands of the world. In Canada, it is the muskeg. In the British Isles, moors. In the United States, we call them bogs and fens. All are only different words for places that have one key trait in common. They are places where the process of decay can't quite keep pace with the process of growth; places of slow and standing water where oxygen levels are too low to effectively break down all the remains of what has died. When something dies in a peatland, be it an Iron Age man, a leaf, or a tree, it adds to the layers of partially decomposed remains that are already there. Most of it will decay, but what does not will build up incrementally in layers over time, reaching a depth of as much as thirty feet. The layers compress under their own weight to make what we call peat and form the basis of a unique and sometimes bizarre community where the dead are as present as the living and the roots of plants on the surface never reach mineral soil.

I walk, on this October day, down a railroad track that runs through a bog not far from Ely, Minnesota. I listen for trains, but there is only the occasional call of a raven, the tapping of a black-backed woodpecker on a dead tree, the high purr of a half dozen cedar waxwings. The sky is clear.

The peatlands of northern Minnesota are part of a complex of boreal peatlands that ring the North Pole in North America, northern Europe, and Siberia. They are here because the last glaciers left behind a landscape of shallow depressions and flatlands where water cannot readily drain away. Their growth is nurtured by a cool continental climate with ample rain and summer temperatures low enough that there is not an excessive loss of surface water from evaporation. Peatland nirvana.

My compass spins in circles, confused by the steel of the railroad tracks until I work my way down the embankment to enter the bog. The landscape before me is blanketed by sphagnum moss and meadows of sedges the color of old burlap with their grasslike leaves bent over into loops. Black spruce trees that look more dead than alive lift their skeletal arms as if beckoning the sky. A rain of needles falls from scattered clusters of tamarack trees turned gold in these shortening days of autumn.

I smile as I remember the words that Colonel William Byrd III wrote in his journal in 1736 about traveling through a peatland. "Never," he said, "was Rum, that cordial of Life, found more necessary than in this Dirty Place." With my first step into the bog, my right leg sinks to midcalf. Fair enough. With my second step, the water comes up, over, and inside my boot. The third step is more complicated. It seems that my right foot is fond of where it is. Would like to stay for a while. Somewhere in the neighborhood of sixteen hundred years. I begin to understand why there hasn't been much in the way of tourism in the peatlands, and why they are considered by some to be the region's last true wilderness.

I extricate my foot. Within a short distance I'm beyond the deep water that rings the bog like a moat and moving gracelessly across the hummocks of green and burgundy sphagnum. It's a little like walking on a trampoline; people have been known to get seasick walking on a bog. The earth gives way beneath my weight. Behind me, I hear the gurgle of water as it rushes back in where my footsteps had displaced it. This place will not miss me when I'm gone.

Peatland communities offer a lean environment for a plant to make a living. As I walk, I know that I tread on nutrients held hostage in the peat—nutrients that the living plants cannot use unless they are set free by the peatland's reluctant process of decay.

The raised surface of the bog and its dense peat base further isolate the plants from the flow of runoff and groundwater. These waters carry dissolved mineral ions that would provide nourishment for plant growth and a buffering of the acids formed within the sphagnum moss. Without them, a bog is left poor in nutrients and high in acids. It is this that distinguishes the two peatland communities termed bogs and fens. A fen, by definition, lies within the path of mineral-laden waters. The surface of a fen is not raised, so it is accessible to runoff. Groundwater that wells to the surface may also travel through the low-lying plants of a fen, bringing a boost of nutrients and bicarbonate or other base from surrounding sediments that buffers the acidity of its waters.

In diversity of species, a fen is considered to be much richer than a bog. Its outside source of sustenance and more alkaline waters allow it to support a greater array of plants. A bog is "fed" only by rain, snowmelt, and what ions the winds can carry from surrounding uplands. Few species of plants can survive in a bog. Even fewer can thrive. Peatlands are often a mosaic of bogs and fens, with the bogs differentiated more by what they lack than what they contain.

Part of the intrigue of a peatland community, be it bog or fen, is the pairing of life and place. As the albatross can soar above the sea for hours without even a flap of its long wings by using the aerodynamic lift created in the friction of air and waves, so too has the life in a peatland found its own way to get along with the conditions it offers.

The black spruce and tamarack I see around me in the bog are able to grow new roots from their trunks and lower branches as the water level rises around them. When high winds throw a black spruce down, upright stems can sprout along the length of the fallen trunk to form new trees. The Labrador tea and leatherleaf plants have waxy and hairy leaf surfaces that may help to prevent the loss of water through evaporation during the extended winters of the north when their roots are ineffective in the frozen peat. Many plants, like the bog rosemary, have small leaves and hang on to them for a long time, saving some of the energy that it takes to produce and maintain them. Others reach beyond a diet of sun and rain. A pitcher plant lies in wait for an insect, nestled in the moss with its palmful of acid cupped in blood-red leaves.

Animals also find a home in the range of habitats offered by these northern bogs and fens, or weave their days between the peatlands and surrounding upland forests. Their presence in and use of the peatlands vary with the season. Sandhill cranes nest in summer in the open fens. Male black bears seek their winter dens in tamarack or black spruce stands. In early spring, the great gray owls wing the spaces between these scattered trees, hooking lemmings and red-backed voles in their talons to feed the owlets that wait in an old raven's nest back in the recesses of the bog.

Northern leopard frogs, spring peepers, wood frogs, and boreal chorus frogs ensure that the peatlands will not lack for song; their reproductive success is greater in the fens, where their eggs fare better in more alkaline waters. Bobcats and coyotes stalk their prey among the moss-covered mounds, and myriad songbirds live and breed in the peatlands. More than a third of Minnesota's species of birds are said to be major users of peatland habitats. Many of them, like the Connecticut and palm warblers, feed on the plentiful supply of insects that bog and fen communities provide.

Where did it begin, I wonder, the notion that a land without people is uninhabited?

I lean over to pick a ripe cranberry from its trailing stem, pop it in my mouth, and cringe at the bite of juice on the back of my tongue. The flavor of bog.

A few days ago, I flew in a small plane over the more than 87,000-square-acre Red Lake Peatland north of Bemidji, Minnesota. The Red Lake Peatland is among the world's most stunning examples of what is called a "patterned peatland."

Unlike the confined peatlands that dwell in small depressions, a patterned peatland forms on broad expanses of flat or gently sloping ground. In the case of the Red Lake Peatland, formed in the ancient bed of glacial Lake Agassiz, the "slope" represents a drop of only one to five feet per mile. Groundwater that seeps up at the upland end of the peatland, along with surface waters contributed by runoff, cannot drain through the impermeable substrate. The water has nowhere to go but to creep downslope at a rate of only a few feet in a week's time, seeking its course as topography and the plants of the peatland allow.

In this setting, in a dynamic and still not fully understood interplay between hydrology, topography, water chemistry, and climate, are created the striking landscape designs for which patterned peatlands are named. They are best seen from the vantage of a bird or a cloud.

The plane passed over Upper Red Lake, the pilot pointing out the wild rice cultivated by farmers along its margins. Then the lake was behind us. What I saw ahead through the dust of that plane's window could well have been the face of another planet.

The features on the surface, though made with a wild hand, were strangely ordered. A vast plain stretched flat and tight as a drum skin out to the circle of the horizon. From it arose islands the shape of teardrops, all oriented with their rounded heads to the west and their trailing tails to the east. Between the teardrops, the surface broke into a phalanx of quavering stripes, broad bands of gold and green that could have been the plow furrows of a farmer with a little too much coffee in his veins. A lone meandering stream and occasional mirrored flash of the sun off the surface were the only visible signs of the water that I knew was moving below the plants as a great, patient river across the landscape.

The illusion was that we were witnessing a suspended parade formation that would begin again as soon as we looked away. But the truth is that it was proceeding as we watched, our sense of time too hurried to perceive its infinitesimal steps.

Science has found names, and reasons, for these patterns. The reasons, like all reasons, are theories. The teardrops are called "tree islands." They are aligned parallel to the flow of water through the peatland and are not islands in the traditional sense of elevated land, but rather are clusters of trees with moss hummocks at their feet. The stripes are alternating pools of water called "flarks" and ridges of peat called "strings" that are dominated by sedges. They run transverse to the migration of water. Tree islands, strings, and flarks form in the channeled water tracks of the Red Lake Peatland that are classified as patterned fens. Their ordered arrangement is thought to be primarily a response of plant growth to the distribution of nutrients carried in the water as it flows. Between the water tracks but out of reach of its nutrients are raised bogs whose forested crests give way to lawns of sphagnum moss.

The roaring of the engine in my ears was nothing compared to the silent roar of the landscape below the plane; in the face of our labels and hard-earned understandings, still inscrutable. Remote.

I had thought that it would feel different here on the ground. Immersed in this musky smell. Standing in the light filtering through humid air. Able to set my feet in the soft moss, to reach my hand down into the peat and close my fist around the living dead in its icy, pulpy mass. Yet it is no less elusive in its very midst, reeking of time and exquisite otherness, the way a longtime lover can suddenly seem less known than is a stranger.

I wonder when the train comes.

The Bog in Summer

Vernal Bogren Swift

I am cutting willow in the boggy part of the field. A worn spot on my tall rubber boots allows the still icy water to pass the membrane of rubber and settle in the tiny lake beds between my toes and into the moat between the castle of my ankle and the boot's inner wall. Because I am standing in midcalf-high bog, the waters inside my boot must ultimately follow the law of physics and rise to the level all around me. It's not a pleasant thought.

Each time I raise my new lake bed, the waters inside slosh, and outside there are sucking sounds when I move. I have lost shoes to this sucking sound before. When I was a child joining my father for the first fishing trip of the spring, our feet would be sucked into the slimy mud banks of the Missouri and Osage Rivers. "Watch for quicksand," we would call to one another, he joking and me serious. Why not quicksand? There's a shoe gone down into that stuff and my bare foot snatched in panic from that shoe and sock and its slide into hell. I know. Exotic images of good people into the quicksand up to their waists before rescue. "Don't move! We'll get you out!" as the good person moans with fear and stays still, so still and still sinking. For the bad guys it was worse. No one around to rescue them, or a rescue too late, or a failure to follow instructions: "Don't move." Until we see, in the final frames showing the event, the nose going under and the brown air bubbles issuing, even as the eyes, the last to go, the eyes frantically seeking escape even as we can imagine the in-rush of mud into the open screaming silent cry, and then that's it. The onlookers, would-be rescuers who have come too late, pause fifteen seconds and then walk out of that terror, looking behind them one last time as they part the swampy green foliage and move on.

What it all comes to is this: these summer nights when the water is high and filled with croakings and unfamiliar creature sounds, it gets a person excited. It gets a person's blood flowing thinner and, on the one hand, makes one want to go outside and down to the willows, and, on the other hand, brings to mind that it might be good to just get a fire permit and dry up all that swamp one of these summer nights. You know, take the mystery out of it. Bring some control back. Too, the crackle of the fire is nice, isn't it? Makes a nice warm backdrop for those moanings and croakings all around us now.

I'm cutting willow. And my foot, the one in the leaking boot, is in complete understanding of its local environment. Already the skin in that place is crinkling and bloodless. In time, if I stay in the lake bed of that boot, the larvae and other vital life in there will blossom and feed from the trunk of my ankle. We will merge life forms in there.

That's what is meant by having an understanding of nature and how things work in it. See, an understanding is just what is going on in this boot. My body's destiny as a pedestrian is undermined by half. One half of me understands this and the other half just squelks along, pulling legs and rubbered feet out of the swamp with the sucking sounds of a two-piston engine in a frail little boat. In times like these, in the dusk of an early spring day, the most elemental part of memory *remembers* that once my kind walked out of the water that was home, and today, she who is still in that home is pulling our leg . . . pulling us back down where she thinks we belong.

If It Rains, They Will Come

Rosalie Hunt Mellor

The day after the Fourth of July, which had been incredibly cold, wet, and dreary, even for northern Minnesota, I sat at my word processor trying vainly to write. Every writer knows those periods when nothing works, so after staring out at the trees writhing in the wind and hearing the intermittent patter of rain, I began to listen. I mean really listen, and I heard voices. They were saying, "If it rains, they will come." I didn't have to ask who "they" were. I knew "they" were mushrooms.

So in rubber boots and raincoat I set forth. Even the dog chose to stay warm and dry in his house, no doubt snickering a little as I sloshed past on my way to the woods where I thought "they" might be. Other than some loathsome-looking witches' butter, which hardly qualifies, it was clear "they" had not come. On my way back I looked into the woods along the path and saw something I had rather expected in such weather: coral mushrooms growing on a rotten log. What I had not expected was something beside them: huge, beautiful white clumps like heads of cauliflower someone had planted and forgotten.

Could it be the rare and delicious cauliflower mushroom? I had found one ten years ago and remembered it well. I took one of the heads in to identify positively, but, to my frustration, it was not the cauliflower mushroom. Similar but not the same. I went through the coral mushrooms but couldn't find this one there, so I kept looking until there it was—a polypore, umbrella polypore, edibility choice.

It is critical to identify mushrooms positively. There is a saying among mushroom hunters: There are old mushroom hunters and bold mushroom hunters, but there are no old, bold mushroom hunters. Bad mushrooms, like the tares in the parable, grow right along with the good ones and may look enough like them to confuse you. Some may only make you nauseated, but the poison in others can do horrible things to your liver or blood cells. This toying with mortality is, I think, part of the mystique of mushrooms, this and the thrill of the chase and the pure aesthetic joy of seeing something wild and pure and lovely with its own reason for being.

When I go in search of those "round tables of the swamp gods," as Thoreau called them, I find more than mushrooms. A grouse explodes from the grass; an astonished timber doodle whirs past like a character out of *Alice in Wonderland,* great long nose and myopic eyes worried and suspicious. It seems to be saying, "Dear me, dear me" as it hurries away. While you may never see it, you will hear the ovenbird shouting its frantic "teacher, teacher, teacher," and the white-throated sparrow sings just one bar of its incredibly sweet song, "old Sam Peabody, Peabody, Peabody," and none of your coaxing will bring it back.

Rarely will you come across another seeker like yourself, for mushroom hunters are as furtive as birds. If you do cross paths, there is no bluff, hearty exchange of "Finding any?" as there might be between fishermen. You tend to avoid each other as if you're concealing some shameful secret, and you slink away and hide behind trees.

The whole experience is mystical and transcendent: the stalk, the uncertainty, the lurking danger. Mushrooms are gathered stealthily, cooked tenderly, given sparingly, and eaten slowly. Otherworldly and utterly unpredictable, their coming and going remains a mystery. To count on them is to depend on stardust and unicorns and leprechauns under hawthorn trees. There are no sure rules. They come when they will and are where they are. For me to say "If it rains, they will come" shames me, for it is to impose my own idea of law and order on the metaphysical. I should say rather that if it rains, they will come if it pleases them, or if that certain tree or bit of ground wants them. They will come if the time is right or if I am ready or if the swamp gods will it.

Part of the experience is in preparing your own senses and soul. If you are looking for them, they are everywhere. Last summer, driving to town for some trivial purchase or some appointment, now long forgotten, I saw oyster mushrooms on dead popples along Highway 2. In spite of rain and fog, I knew what I saw. "Stop, stop," I shouted. "Oyster mushrooms." My daughter, who was driving, braked smartly and pulled out on the shoulder. I had the door open before the car stopped and we darted across the highway, dodging cars and soaking our shoes, for the trees stood in water, but the oysters were prime and we filled sacks with our fragrant, succulent treasure.

In the fall after rains, we look for shaggymanes on a certain wide, well-manicured public lawn. They come unannounced, popping up overnight and spreading across the bright green grass like a drift of snow. Time is of the essence with shaggymanes. Of the inky cap family, they will dissolve into a dark slime within hours. They must be gathered and cooked within minutes or they turn pink and then brown and nasty—and taste the way they look.

Mushroom season begins with the first spring rains and ends with the serious frosts of late fall. Morel, oyster, meadow, fairy ring, chanterelle, puffball, bear's head, and shaggymane are a few of the varieties you can find outside your door, many even in the city. The inscrutable world of mushrooms harks back to ancient laws and lore largely forgotten in our plastic, ready-made times. If oak leaves are the size of a mouse's ear or if trilliums push up by a certain elm tree, go where the timber doodle rushes by consulting his pocket watch, and if it rains, they will come.

Longing for Little Trout

Margaret A. Haapoja

The flutelike notes of a red-winged blackbird never fail to conjure up memories of my first fishing trip to Little Trout Lake. A willing neophyte, I was introduced to camping by my husband-to-be back in the days when chaperones were a prudent requirement. My parents accompanied us on that outing, and on many others thereafter.

Just north of one of Lake Vermilion's jagged arms, Big Trout Lake lies on the far side of a long portage. Due north and slightly west of Big Trout is Little Trout, our destination. These sister lakes are connected by a narrow creek that twists through shallow marshland. This and other Boundary Waters Canoe Area portages have been the focus of a tug-of-war between special interest groups.

Beyond this portage, Little Trout holds deep water and the beginnings of my marriage. It is still there, oblivious to its own significance in our history and hearts or its meanings in courtrooms, newspapers, and coffee shop controversy.

Our sixty-horse motor was bought and paid for before our children were born—an extravagant luxury for a young couple. Just months after we completed the only trip we ever took there with our two children, it felt as if the U.S. Forest Service robbed us of the opportunity to revisit Little Trout Lake as a family: a new law limited outboard motor size to twenty-five horsepower. Even with tight penny-pinching, a new rig was not in our budget.

With the closing of the Trout Lake portage to motorized transportation a couple of years ago, we are now effectively shut out for good. We travel to our favorite fishing hole on Little Trout Lake only in memory, and we lament what we have lost.

To reach our destination on those long-ago trips, we put into Lake Vermilion, ran up the rocky edge of the lake several miles, and loaded our boat onto an ancient flatbed truck. The truck portage—about a mile and a half across—was part of the adventure. The driver was a perennially familiar figure. We clung to the truck bunk's sides, bracing ourselves against the boat to keep it from sliding off on bumps and sharp corners. Our black Labrador, Dinah, enjoyed the experience as much as we did, racing behind and making brief forays into the woods on either side, hot on the trail of some varmint or another.

The scent of balm of Gilead was sharp in our nostrils as we rode along. Often we sensed, rather than heard, the persistent thrumming of a partridge not far away. Early woodland wildflowers— hepatica, marsh marigolds, and false lily of the valley—embroidered the edges of the roadway, a treat for winter-weary eyes. A blizzard of blossoms swirled around us as the truck brushed the branches of a wild plum in full bloom.

When we reached the other side of the portage, the driver removed the tires wedged beneath the boat and backed the truck slowly into the water, brakes squealing every foot of the way. When he was satisfied with the depth of the water, he stopped the truck, clambered onto the truck bed. With the help of any men present, he boosted the boat into the lake. We were ready to continue the journey.

Big Trout Lake lives up to its name and our memories. Several miles long and wide, very deep in spots, it can be treacherous when the wind is strong. There were times when our deep-V runabout had all it could handle to navigate these waters safely. I shudder to think of crossing in a canoe when the weather is rough. But on clear, calm days there are few lakes lovelier. Sheer rock cliffs tower over the water, and virgin white pines stand as silent sentinels along the shore.

Visits to Little Trout became an annual rite with each mid-May opener. One year—more than twenty-five years ago—we left home in a late spring snowstorm, hopeful and determined. Everything seemed frustratingly late that year and the ice still covered the lakes. Launching our boat at Moccasin Point as usual, we traveled up Lake Vermilion as far as we could until a wall of ice blocked the way. Still hopeful the ice would shift by morning, we made camp for the night and slept in warm sleeping bags with our fingers crossed. Our hopes were dashed when we awoke, and we were forced to find another fishing spot that weekend. We returned the following Saturday to open water and caught the biggest stringer of walleyes we've seen in a lifetime of fishing, including one beauty weighing nearly eleven pounds.

The entrance into Little Trout Lake is tricky—a narrow, winding, shallow creek. To maneuver safely, Don would move aft in the boat and lift the large motor out of the water so he could operate the small motor manually. Below us boulders flashed with the aluminum scrapes left by many other boats. I perched high on the prow pointing out rocks to avoid. Turtles slid silently from submerged logs. Delicate blossoms of Labrador tea scented the air. Minnows darted in and out of the reeds ahead of us. Red-winged blackbirds teetered on the tops of cattails, trilling the plaintive song I would later realize was a prelude to the loss of these days.

As we neared the widening in the channel that led out into the lake, the sun sparkled on the lake's surface, and we spotted our favorite campsite. If we were in luck, no one had claimed it before us. For many years we set up our tent on the lone island, its natural harbor sheltering the boat, its rocky point perfect for early-morning casts.

One evening on that island we looked forward to a fine meal of barbecued steak. As we waited for the coals to reach the red hot stage, we reminisced about past fishing trips. Finally it was time to grill. I went to retrieve the steaks I'd left defrosting on the picnic table. There sat Dinah licking her chops. We ate fish.

When the twenty-five-horsepower law took effect, we began to look for new territory. Canada coaxed us across the border with the lure of unrestricted remote lakes. Don and I always shared the thought that perhaps we were born too late to satisfy our lust for wilderness. Our romance with wild places pulled us farther north. The air seemed cleaner, the sky more blue, the water, pristine.

We tried a Florida vacation to substitute something new for places that were becoming difficult to reach. We were nearly overwhelmed by bumper-to-bumper traffic, long lines, and too many bodies on the beaches. We were disappointed to find almost no oceanfront in its natural state and public access always limited. Palatial estates and high-rise condominiums have gobbled up every square inch of sand. After two weeks, we longed for the wilderness of border lakes.

Through thirty years of marriage, we sought solitude in the north country with the same determination we've sought to understand one another. When we were younger, we canoed Canada's lakes, portaging as far from civilization as we could manage in a four-day weekend. We tented on Beaverhouse, Cirrus, and Jean. We made the acquaintance of lakes with exotic, beckoning Indian names like Otukamamoan, Kenozhe, Kawawia, and Kaopskikamak.

The first time I made a canoe trip, I couldn't believe the amount of physical labor involved. I found myself thinking, "And this is supposed to be fun?" Although I've never carried a canoe, I've lugged heavy Duluth packs, loaded coolers, outboard motors, minnow buckets, sleeping bags, tents, and tackle boxes.

On perfect days, all the planning, preparation, and packing paid off. At the end of the last portage, we'd slide the canoe into calm waters. No cabins cluttered the shoreline, and there were few campers to disturb the silence. Several shades of green wove a patchwork quilt against the distant horizon. Dark-needled pines contrasted with shiny aspen leaves and bronze viburnum bushes. Dense undergrowth down to the water's edge made the woods nearly impenetrable. Inside, plush moss carpet muffled our footsteps and provided a cushion from which to kneel and pick blueberries. Loon calls lingered on the air and mating mergansers flew overhead. We once watched a pair of young otters at play, later claiming their crescent-shaped beach for the rest of a hot afternoon. The sand was soft on our bare feet, and yellow beaver cuttings littered the shore. A haphazardly stacked pile of clam shells was evidence of some creature's delectable meal.

From the time our two children were toddlers, we took them along on camping trips. They learned to sit patiently on boat cushions in the bottom of the canoe. They helped cut firewood and gathered wildflowers for the table's centerpiece. They pitched rocks into rivers and lost fishing rods in lakes. They were there when midnight visitors, a mother bear and two cubs, smelled fish entrails from a day's catch, and when we lost an entire stringer of walleyes to hungry turtles. More than once we watched in wonder as a changing kaleidoscope of northern lights shimmered across the summer sky. We sought to instill in Tom and Amy our love for the unspoiled lands of the north.

On one such trip, we found an old log cabin, lonesome and overgrown with weeds and moss. We peeked through cracked windowpanes to see a thin-mattressed bed, a rusted stove, and broken dishes—sad evidence of the dreams of a trapper from a distant time. The scene animated my father's stories of his own youth—of winters spent in a cabin not unlike this one—when he'd trapped beaver and mink for a living and an adventure.

We are older now, and our mode of travel has changed with the years. Back surgery made portaging difficult for Don, and tenting has lost some of its appeal. For many years we've traveled in our pickup camper, making day trips by canoe.

In retirement, we fish in comfort from resorts and outpost cabins on Pipestone, Lake of the Woods, Sand Point, Lac La Croix, and Lac Seul. Conceding some solitude, we still escape the crowded campgrounds farther south. Adventure now is to reach a quiet backwater where remnants of log booms float. We can still find an isolated bay where ospreys nest. We hope a lunker lake trout lurks in the waters we fish. We remember the trips of our youth and the places we can no longer reach.

Northern Passages

Sam Cook

My early northern passages were made with paddle and packsack, or on the runners of a dogsled or a pair of cross-country skis.

I was new in this country—the North Woods—and I couldn't get enough of it. I wanted to fill in the blank spots on my maps, make the portages I had heard about, follow rivers to Hudson Bay, know how it feels to sleep under the shimmer of northern lights.

My partners and I were drawn sometimes by the promise of walleyes or lake trout, but just as often by the sheer adventure of seeing what was around the next bend.

We did find some walleyes and lake trout. We made camps where the spirit of the voyageurs danced in our fires. We came to know mosquitoes and blackflies, good sled dogs and cold nights, wild rivers and big lakes.

The passages weren't always easy. At times we found ourselves thigh deep in bogs, or desperate for the lee of the next island on a windswept lake or pushing after dark behind a team of dogs. But it didn't matter. We were young people in new country, and we weren't pushing ourselves so much as we were being pulled along by the country itself.

Now, though, some of that has changed. Our passages aren't always those of the paddle and path. Instead they're the passages of life: having children, waking up and finding ourselves in the middle of life, watching friendships mature, wondering what the years ahead hold for us.

When we had our first child a few years ago, I remember telling friends that, no, our lives haven't changed. We still camp. We still fish. We still paddle and portage.

That much was true. We do many of the things we once did, but we do them for different reasons. At a different pace. With new rewards.

One thing hasn't changed. We're still experiencing these new passages in our lives against the backdrop of the north. It means something to me that our six-year-old knows the call of the barred owl, that she reports with excitement each April that the peepers are peeping again, that she can fall asleep as easily in a canoe as in her own bed.

I find, these days, all of that matters more than whether I have caught walleyes.

I never thought it would be this way. I never thought I'd find myself four days into a weeklong trip and fighting an intense desire to be at home, rocking a one-year-old to bed.

It never occurred to me that going back to a familiar camp on a familiar lake with a good friend would mean as much to me as coming to know a new piece of the map. But it does.

Passages. They slip up on you like a morning fog on a canoe-country lake in September. Like a full moon, there, before you know it, over Lake Superior. Like the smell of wood smoke, drifting down the lake from your camp when you're paddling back at dusk.

I'm not sure what new discoveries are ahead of me. I'm not sure

I'll be ready for them, or that I'll even recognize them as they unfold.

But I think I know how I'll find them. I'll be shuffling along some portage trail, trying to appreciate a patch of bunchberries while the yoke of the canoe bites into my shoulders. I'll be sliding into a cold sleeping bag on a February night, listening to sled dogs jangling the stakeout chain outside the tent. I'll be gazing up from the water at a cluster of Indian rock paintings, marveling at this country that has changed so little in so many centuries.

That's where I'll be. Finding new passages. Here in the north.

Traveling Light

Susan Hawkinson

Taking a canoe trip is the freest I ever feel. Everything my partner and I need for the next nine days is in the canoe. Adequate food but not extra, a lightweight compact stove and ration of fuel, two small pots, two cups, two teaspoons, a stirring spoon and jackknife, two paddles with a spare, a tent and tarp, a few changes of clothing, rain gear and life jackets. No saw, shovel, or frying pan. No rod, bait, or fish batter. A slim book, a small notepad, a pen. And, of course, the maps.

The last several trips we have cut cooking to boiling water for coffee and cereal in the morning and for a thin soup of dried vegetables at night. During the day, we consume high-energy snacks like dried fruits and nuts, peanut butter and jam on hardtack. Since I know the calories we need to paddle and portage, I know we each drop a thousand calories a day, two pounds total, yet never go hungry. We choose to lose this weight not because we need to but because we can travel lighter. Perhaps that's why I feel so much freer on canoe trips. Each day there literally is a little less of me.

In camp, we don't clean blackened pots and pans, earlier balanced on stones over a cooking fire, which I did as a young canoer. Those dawns and dusks down by the water, squatting, scrubbing, and muttering about the cook who did not soap the outside of the pot, are bygone days. Instead we rinse the faintest film of soup from our pan, then wash our cups and spoons.

Mornings, I sit on a rock near the water's edge allowing my thoughts to tumble into undisturbed or faintly rippling clouds and birch reflected in the lake. No fire to stoke, no pot to stir. I lose whatever's left of me in that deep place I've worn myself out trying to paddle to. Evenings, it is the same. After supper, my thoughts move out among the branches of the trees, latticework to cradle stars, another mix of sky and clouds and forest. Again I am gone to a different darker space of letting go.

We talk less in canoe country, no longer interrupt the natural sounds of creaking trees and pounding waves with the sound of our own voices. Listening to wind and shore and water, I find out once more where I fit. It is a shrinking of self, an emptying of ego, an enlarging of the natural world. Awe courses through my blood and bones but not across my lips.

Traveling light, I do not think of evening camp, setting up tent and tarp, cooking supper before dark. We are not monitored by wristwatches. Ours is not a time-consuming process. It is a time-releasing process. We travel by the urging of our bodies, resting when we're tired, eating when we're hungry, no longer calling the hours of the day by name. Our units for dividing life grow larger.

When we leave the lakes to drive home, fewer thoughts click through my head. I don't see the future in the scenery passing by; nothing reminds me of things I have to do. I see the here and now here and now. It is my summer housecleaning, a getting rid of what I do not need. I am lighter, freer; in fact, this is the freest I ever feel.

By the Fire

Douglas Wood

The day is easing into night, dishes are done, wet shoes sizzle by the campfire. Probably ought to move them back a bit. Or at least turn them. Nah, they're okay. For a little while, at least.

I remember waiting too long, once, on a spring fishing trip. I got a good blaze going in a tennis shoe. One of the guys remarked, "I believe your shoe is on fire." It was. I grabbed it by the toe and heaved it toward the lake. It made a long fiery arc across the night sky, trailing a tail like a meteor, and hit the water with a nice *fz-z-z-z-z.*

We all admired the beauty of it.

I had to paddle out and get the shoe. (It floated.) Sitting out there off the shore, in the gathering gloom, I was struck by the profound beauty of . . . something—of a delicate sliver of moon sliding down a western slope of sky, of dark pinnacle spruce and emerging stars and their reflections in the quicksilver lake, and of the picture that included all these things. And at the center of the picture, three silhouetted forms gathered around a dancing orange flame.

I watched for a long time.

Is there anything more fascinating than a campfire, anything that has drawn and held human attention so gently, so firmly, for so long? The enchantment of a fire is easily forgotten in the rush of modern existence, yet it never completely disappears. The spark of fascination remains, and can be quickly kindled back to life in a quiet moment before a campfire, a fireplace, or a woodstove, even a candle. Suddenly the rush stops, a calm descends, and there is time to contemplate. So universal is this intuitive response that nearly every religion or spiritual tradition makes central use of the flame or the candle in meditation or ritual, a symbol of mysteries honored from time immemorial.

There are times and places when a campfire is not appropriate, when we must go softly and leave no trace. At such times the crackle of logs is replaced by the hiss of a propane stove. The food gets just as warm, and probably faster. The scenery is as lovely, the companionship fine, and there is no charcoal on the hands or smoke in the eyes. But there is something important missing—the punctuation mark at the end of the day, the magnet that draws eyes and minds and provides a center of repose and reflection. The camp stove, functional as it is, can never be a fire in the same sense that a campfire is.

Sometimes a campfire is a time for celebration, a catalyst for jokes and songs and, of course, stories. Something about the hypnotic dance of the flames triggers memories, and tales are told and retold and embellished until they are woven into a brightly colored fabric of imagination. Inevitably such evenings reach a climax of hilarity and foolishness, then begin to fade into the silence of the night as the campfire is allowed to die. The flames grow smaller, half-burned logs are kicked into the still-burning center, attention focuses on inward thoughts and feelings. There is a quiet that no one cares to break.

Late on one such night in the Quetico, when silence had descended and the last blue and yellow flames flickered, we heard a sound. It came from the darkness out on the lake, a sound straight out of the past, out of the fabric of imagination and fantasy we had woven around the campfire that evening, as we talked about the voyageurs of old. Wide-eyed glances at one another confirmed we'd all heard it, the sound of voyageurs singing an old French chanson, a paddling song. It drifted eerily through the dark, faintly at first, then growing clearer. Soon we could actually hear the fast-paced strokes of paddles slicing and gurgling in the water as the singing grew louder and louder.

Suddenly came a sharp command—"Whoa!"—just as the canoe reached the faint edge of our firelight by the shore. Paddles jammed into the water, and the canoe stopped abruptly. No one around our circle had moved. Eyes were still wide, hearts racing. Then came the voice again. "Hey, you guys seen Jack?"

We had not seen Jack. As it turned out, neither had we heard, or met, ghost voyageurs out of the past, but instead three young guys from a lodge eight miles and a long portage distant. They were out for a midnight lark, just looking to say hi to a buddy. Another time we might have known, wouldn't have been fooled for even a moment. But by the spell of the campfire . . . well, those fellows were voyageurs out of the past whether they knew it or not. And the way they sang and paddled, they could have been.

Night has always seemed the time of the most memorable campfires, for the magic they can bring. The air is thick then with the smells of the woods, the ground stretched a little more loosely and comfortably over the bones of the earth. Forgotten dreams are abroad, moving over the shadowy landscape of the mind. It's a time for thinking differently, for seeing differently than in the cold light of day. Dreams are built, plans laid, lives examined, and sometimes things are seen more clearly than ever before.

People build fires for different reasons. Some people like a roaring blaze, to keep the night at bay; the campfire is security, light, protection from the unknown in a new and strange place. For others, it begins as a project, a reason to stay busy "doing," gathering tinder, breaking sticks and twigs, splitting logs. But eventually the fire always becomes the still center, a mirror of personal reflection. I'll never forget the way Gene taught me to look at a campfire. We had been still a long time when eventually I reached a foot over and moved a log a little bit. "You killed my flame," he said, slightly accusingly. "What do you mean?" I answered, suspecting he'd had a little extra Yukon Jack.

"I like to pick out one flame," he said, "and make it my own. I focus on it and watch everything it does, changing colors, growing bigger, maybe moving over and catching the twig or branch next to it. I watch it until it disappears completely. Haven't you ever done that?"

Well, I do now. Sometimes. Sometimes I gaze into a fire and see Gene, or others who have shared other campfires. Sometimes I see my granddad, who's been gone twenty-five years, but who kindled in me a spark that grew into a burning love for the outdoors and wild places.

And sometimes I just dry my shoes.

Hmm . . . I really ought to move that one back now. It's steaming pretty good. Or is that smoke? Of course I could just let it catch fire and then heave it out into the lake—just for old time's sake. It'd be real pretty.

Contributors

Laurie Allmann is the author of *Far from Tame: Reflections from the Heart of a Continent* (Minnesota, 1996). She has been a regularly featured essayist and commentator for Minnesota Public Radio's *Voices from the Heartland* series, and selections of her poetry have been published in the *Floating Fish Quarterly Review*. She has adapted her writing for the stage in performances at the Playwrights Center and the Southern Theater in Minneapolis. Her professional background includes work as a wilderness canoe guide and naturalist. Allmann was born in Jordan, Minnesota, and now writes from her home in the St. Croix River Valley.

Elnora Bixby worked as a nurse in her native Baudette, Minnesota, for twenty-eight years while she was raising three children. She is the author of *North of Nowhere,* a collection of essays. She retired from nursing in 1986 and now observes nature with her husband at their home near Lake of the Woods.

Roger K. Blakely, a native of Barnum, Minnesota, was an air force cryptographer in India and the western Pacific theater during World

War II and returned to teach English, American literature, and art history at his alma mater, Macalester College in St. Paul. He is the author of *North from Duluth* and *Wolfgang Amadeus Mozart* and coeditor of *Stillers Pond*.

Carol Bly was born in Duluth, Minnesota, and currently divides her time between Sturgeon Lake, Minnesota, and St. Paul. She is the author of several books, including *Letters from the Country*, *Backbone*, *The Tomcat's Wife and Other Stories*, and *Changing the Bully Who Rules the World*. Bly teaches creative writing in the summer Split Rock Program, in the Lifelong Learning Program of Northland College, and at the University of Minnesota.

Jim Brandenburg is a natural history photographer and filmmaker whose work has been published in the *New York Times*, *Life*, *Audubon*, *Smithsonian*, *Natural History*, *National Wildlife*, *Outside*, and many other national and international publications. He is the author of many books, including *Brother Wolf: A Forgotten Promise*, *White Wolf: Living with an Arctic Legend*, and *Minnesota: Images of Home*.

Sam Cook is the author of the award-winning outdoor series *Up North*, *Quiet Magic,* and *CampSights*. He also shares his insights and observations through his weekly columns in the *Duluth News-Tribune*. A native of Kansas, Cook now lives in Duluth, Minnesota, with his wife, Phyllis, and their children, Emily and Grant.

Pauline Brunette Danforth grew up on the White Earth Reservation in northern Minnesota and in Minneapolis. She graduated from Bemidji State University and is currently pursuing a Ph.D. in American studies at the University of Minnesota.

Marlon Davidson is a visual artist and writer whose graphic works are held in both public and private collections. A published poet, Davidson was educated at Bemidji State University and the Minneapolis College of Art and Design. His short story *Thinking of Samson* appeared in the *James White Review*.

Steven R. Downing lives in Grand Rapids, Minnesota. He has published both short fiction and nonfiction and is a regular columnist for the *Duluth News-Tribune*. His political essays and dramas have been produced for public radio. He is currently at work on a novel.

Anne M. Dunn is an Ojibwe grandmother, descended on her mother's side from the Mississippi Band of that nation. She was born in 1940 at Red Lake and currently resides on the nearby Leech Lake Reservation in northern Minnesota near the town of Cass Lake. She writes a column for *The Circle,* a Minneapolis American Indian newspaper, and publishes a monthly newsletter of traditional tales and social commentary, *The Beaver Tail Times.*

Anne Marie Erickson lives north of Deer River, Minnesota, in a log house she and her husband built. They lived and taught in Madrid, Spain, for a year and now have a home-based writing, photography, and graphic design business. A graduate of Augsburg College in Minneapolis, Erickson has three adult stepchildren.

Jeanne Grauman is a student at Itasca Community College in Grand Rapids, Minnesota. Born and raised on a northern Minnesota farm, she is the mother of three and has been happily married for twenty-one years.

Bobbie Greiner and her husband, Jim, divide their time and energies between their backwoods cabin and their home and jobs in International Falls, Minnesota. In addition to writing a nonfiction work in progress, from which "From the Rio Grande to the Rainy" is an excerpt, Greiner is currently marketing a novel she completed in 1995.

Margaret A. Haapoja is a native Iron Ranger and a freelance writer. She writes a biweekly garden column for the *Grand Rapids Herald-Review,* and her articles have appeared in *Harrowsmith Country Review*, *Country Journal, Horticulture, Country Home, Flower and Garden, Modern Maturity, New Choices, Kiwanis, Log Home Living, American Forests, Minnesota Monthly, Lake Superior*, and *Minnesota Volunteer.*

She and her husband built their home on Little Sand Lake south of Calumet, Minnesota, more that twenty-five years ago.

Susan Carol Hauser, an essayist and poet. Her books include *Nature's Revenge: The History of Poison Ivy, Poison Oak, Poison Sumac, and Their Remedies, Meant to Be Read Out Loud,* which received a 1989 Minnesota Book Award, and *Girl to Woman: A Gathering of Images.*

Susan Hawkinson, an English instructor at Itasca Community College in Grand Rapids, Minnesota, has read her essays on her local community radio station, KAXE. For more than twenty-five years she has paddled the canoe wilderness in northern Minnesota and Canada.

John Henricksson is a writer and editor who divides his time between Mahtomedi, Minnesota, and his Gunflint Lake cabin. He is the author of *Rachel Carson: The Environmental Movement* and editor of *North Writers: A Strong Woods Collection* (Minnesota, 1991).

Jim dale Huot-Vickery is a native of northwestern Minnesota's Red River Valley. He is the author of *Wilderness Visionaries* and *Open Spaces,* which won the Sigurd Olson Nature Writing Award in 1992. He has worked as a freelance author, as a Quetico-Superior canoe trip guide, teacher, lecturer, and as a National Park Service ranger in the Apostle Islands of Lake Superior.

Justine Kerfoot was born in Great Barrington, Illinois, in 1906. She moved to Gunflint Lake in 1928 and was the owner-operator of the Gunflint Lodge for fifty-one years. She is the author of *Woman of the Boundary Waters* (Minnesota, 1994) and *Gunflint* and has written a weekly column for the *Cook County News-Herald* since 1956.

Jim Klobuchar's forty-three years in journalism include thirty years as a columnist for the *Star-Tribune* of Minneapolis. From mountaintops to the floors of political conventions, he has always written about the human condition from the perspective of a native son of the Iron

Range. In 1984 Klobuchar was named the nation's outstanding columnist by the National Society of Newspaper Columnists. He is also the author of fourteen books.

Peter M. Leschak is a freelance writer who lives in northeastern Minnesota. His books include *Letters from Side Lake* (Minnesota, 1992), *The Bear Guardian*, which won a Minnesota Book Award, *Seeing the Raven* (Minnesota, 1994), and *The Snow Lotus* (Minnesota, 1996). He is also a freelance wildland firefighter and works fires across the United States for various state and federal agencies.

Rosalie Hunt Mellor retired to northern Minnesota after a career teaching English in Iowa and Michigan. She lives in a house at the end of the road, travels by horse and canoe whenever possible, and spends her days writing and reflecting near the loon-nested banks of Blackberry Lake.

Matthew Miltich teaches English at Itasca Community College. He lives with his wife, Loree, and their children on Dear North Farm near Grand Rapids, Minnesota, in the same county in which he was born and raised.

Sharon Miltich teaches English at Fergus Falls Community College. She grew up in LaPrairie, Minnesota, and left the Iron Range in 1984. Miltich has a master of arts degree from Bemidji State University, where her thesis, "A Range of Voices: Literature of Minnesota's Mesabi Range," was awarded a prize for outstanding scholarly work by a graduate student. She lives with her husband and three children in Fergus Falls, Minnesota.

Kent Nerburn holds a Ph.D. in religion and art and is the editor of three books of Native American speeches and writings. He is the author of *Letters to My Son* and *Neither Wolf nor Dog: On Forgotten Roads with an Indian Elder*, which won the Minnesota Book Award in 1995. "Burial" is excerpted from Nerburn's *A Haunting Reverence: Meditations on a Northern Land* (1996).

Sheila Packa is a poet and fiction writer who lives in Duluth, Minnesota. Her work has appeared in *Ploughshares* and other literary magazines. She has a master of fine arts degree in creative writing and has received two Loft McKnight Awards, one in poetry and one in prose.

Donna Salli was born and raised along the Wisconsin-Michigan border. She earned a master of fine arts degree in poetry from the University of Massachusetts at Amherst and has studied with numerous poets.

Jana Studelska lives in Ely, Minnesota, with her family, working as a freelance writer.

Barton Sutter has lived in Duluth, Minnesota, since 1987. He is the author of *The Book of Names,* which won the Minnesota Book Award for Poetry in 1994, and *My Father's War and Other Stories*, which won the Minnesota Book Award for Fiction in 1992.

Vernal Bogren Swift lives with Eric Bogren on a former dairy farm outside Bovey, Minnesota. Dry when they bought it, the land has since returned to wetlands. She likes it that way.

Robert Treuer lives on a tree farm near Bemidji, Minnesota. The Vienna-born Holocaust survivor has been a union journalist and organizer, teacher, community organizer on reservations, and government official. He is also the author of numerous books, essays, articles, and short stories.

Jane Whitledge's poems and essays have appeared in a number of magazines and literary journals including *Yankee, Wilderness, Bird Watcher's Digest, A View from the Loft, Kansas Quarterly, North Stone Review, South Coast Poetry Journal*, and many others. She lives near Winton, Minnesota.

Douglas Wood is the author of the classic best-selling fable *Old Turtle*, winner of the 1993 ABBY Award and the International Reading Association's Book of the Year Award. He writes and composes music in his log cabin homes, one north of St. Cloud, Minnesota, on the Mississippi River, the other on an island in Rainy Lake.

Permissions and Publication Histories

Laurie Allmann, "Sand Lake Peatland, October," from *Far from Tame: Reflections from the Heart of a Continent*, published by the University of Minnesota Press, 1996, copyright 1996 by Laurie Allmann, reprinted by permission.

Elnora Bixby, "Everyone Talks about It," originally appeared in *North of Nowhere: A Collection of Essays* published by Williams Northern Light, 1989, copyright 1989 by Elnora Bixby.

Roger K. Blakely, "Breaking the Ribbon," originally appeared in *North from Duluth* published by New Rivers Press, 1981.

Carol Bly, "At the Edge of Town: Duluth, Minn.," from *Townships*, edited by Michael Martone, published by the University of Iowa Press, 1992, reprinted by permission.

Jim Brandenburg, "In the Company of Wolves," from *Brother Wolf: A Forgotten Promise* (as adapted for publication in *National Wildlife* [December/January 1995]), published by NorthWord Press, Inc., 1993, copyright 1993 by Jim Brandenburg, reprinted by permission of the author.

Sam Cook, "Northern Passages," from *CampSights*, published by Pfeifer-Hamilton, 1992, copyright 1992 by Sam Cook, reprinted by permission.

Anne M. Dunn, "Sugar Bush," from *When Beaver Was Very Great: Stories to Live By*, published by Midwest Traditions, Inc., 1995, copyright 1995 by Anne M. Dunn, reprinted by permission.

Susan Hawkinson, "Traveling Light," previously published in *Community Connections* 9, no. 3 (Summer 1995).

227

Tom Hennen, "Love for Other Things," copyright 1993 by Tom Hennen and Dacotah Territory Press, reprinted by permission.

Jim dale Huot-Vickery, excerpt from *Open Spaces*, published by NorthWord Press, Inc., 1991, copyright 1991 by Jim dale Vickery, reprinted by permission.

Justine Kerfoot, "Ice Harvest," excerpted from *Woman of the Boundary Waters: Canoeing, Guiding, Mushing, and Surviving*, published by the University of Minnesota Press, 1994, copyright 1986, 1994 by Justine Kerfoot, reprinted by permission.

Jim Klobuchar, "The Red Dirt Ennobled Their Faces," from *Eight Miles without a Pothole: As Close to Heaven as I'm Going to Get,* published by Voyageur Press, Inc., 1986, copyright 1986 by Jim Klobuchar, reprinted by permission.

Peter M. Leschak, "Chickadee Bob," from *Seeing the Raven: A Narrative of Renewal*, published by the University of Minnesota Press, 1994, copyright 1994 by Peter M. Leschak, reprinted by permission.

Donna Salli, "Women in the Wood Smoke," originally appeared in *Mpls.St. Paul* (February 1994).

Vernel Bogren Swift, "The Bog in Summer," originally appeared in *Community Connections* (Summer 1994), published by the Minnesota Project.

Robert Treuer, "Finding Symmetry in a Rock Pile," from *A Northwoods Window*, published by Voyageur Press, Inc., 1990, copyright 1990 by Robert Treuer, reprinted by permission of the author.

Jane Whitledge, "Wild Goose Chase," originally appeared in *Bird Watchers Digest* (January/February 1994).

Douglas Wood, "By the Fire," originally appeared in *Canoe* (May 1990).